HORRIBLE SCIENCE

SOUNDS DREADFUL

NICK ARNOLD

Illustrated by
Tony De Saulles

Hippo

Other titles in this series include:
Ugly Bugs
Blood, Bones and Body Bits
Chemical Chaos
Nasty Nature
Fatal Forces
Disgusting Digestion

Scholastic Children's Books,
Commonwealth House, 1-19 New Oxford Street,
London WC1A 1NU, UK
A division of Scholastic Ltd
London ~ New York ~ Toronto ~ Sydney ~ Auckland

First published in the UK by Scholastic Ltd, 1998

ISBN 0 590 19810 6

Typeset by Rapid Reprographics Ltd, London.
Printed by Cox & Wyman Ltd, Reading, Berks.

10 9 8 7 6 5 4 3 2 1

Contents

Introduction   5

Sounding off   8

Dreadful hearing   21

Speedy sound waves   40

Shattering sounds   60

Noisy nature   69

Eerie echoes   78

Dreadful body sounds   92

Dreadful musical mayhem   114

Dreadful sound effects   133

Rotten recordings   144

Sounding it out   156

YO! A SCIENCE BOOK!
SOUNDS DREADFUL?
SOUNDS COOL TO ME, MAN!

Nick Arnold has been writing stories and books since he was a youngster, but never dreamt he'd find fame writing about dreadful sound. His research involved singing in the bath, shouting at the top of his voice and trying to decipher the lyrics to pop songs and he enjoyed every minute of it.

When he's not delving into Horrible Science, he spends his spare time teaching adults in a college. His hobbies include eating pizza, riding his bike and thinking up corny jokes (though not all at the same time).

Tony De Saulles picked up his crayons when he was still in nappies and has been doodling ever since. He takes Horrible Science very seriously and even agreed to investigate if snakes have ears. Fortunately, his injuries weren't too serious.

When he's not out with his sketchpad, Tony likes to write poetry and play squash, though he hasn't written any poetry about squash yet.

((((INTRODUCTION))))

Listen to this...

The younger you are, the LOUDER you are. Babies love making noise...

And so do kids...

And teenagers think really loud music is **brilliant!**

But as people grow older they change. They settle down

and quieten down. Your parents no longer think LOUD is good. They think that anything LOUD sounds dreadful. Especially loud sounds made by YOU!

So you'd better read this book *q-u-i-e-t-l-y*.
And guess what? Teachers are *even* worse.

In fact, the only sound teachers seem to enjoy is the sound of their own voices. Sounding off about boring things. Like science, for example. And just to put you off the idea of making noise – teachers teach you about sound in science.

Sounds dreadful, doesn't it? But it doesn't have to be…

Listen to a few more exciting sound facts and see if they make your ears prick up:

• A single note can shatter glass.

• Sound makes your eyeballs shiver in their sockets.

• Sound stuns and even kills people.

And that's not all. This book is full of facts about a world of dreadful sounds – from bells that can burst your blood vessels, to sinister sound guns that can make you dash for the toilet. Read all about it and afterwards you can sound off in science class to your heart's content. You're bound to get a good hearing.

And who knows? You could become a big noise in science. One thing's for sure – the world will never sound the same to you again. So now that you're all ears, just turn the page…

SOUNDING OFF

What do the following have in common?
a) Your pet mouse
b) Your science teacher
c) A sixty-piece orchestra
Give up?
No, the answer *isn't* that they all eat cheese. The correct answer is they all use *sound* to grab your attention. The orchestra needs sound to play a symphony, the mouse needs sound to squeak and your science teacher ... well, just imagine there was no such thing as sound. You couldn't listen to a boring science lesson. And she'd never get to tell you off. That would be tragic!

For animals sound is equally vital because, just like us, animals use sound to pass on vital messages. Just imagine what would happen if your dog couldn't whimper when it was time to go out for "walkies". You might forget to take him out...

SILENT MESSAGE

SMELLY MESSAGE

TIME FOR WALKIES!

Speak like a scientist
Scientists have their very own language which only they understand. Now's your chance to learn a few key words.

And afterwards you can sound off and amaze your friends and silence your teacher with your word-power.

Enormous AMPLITUDE (am-plee-tude)

This means how loud a sound is. Stronger sound waves mean louder sounds, or greater amplitude. The word amplitude comes from "ample" which also means BIG. Got that?

HIGH AMPLITUDE SOUND WAVES (BIG SOUND = BIG SOUND WAVE)

AMPLE SCIENTIST

CHEW GOBBLE SCOFF MUNCH

AMPLE DINNER

Fantastic FREQUENCY

Frequency means the number of vibrations a second that make up a sound. These can be incredibly fast. For example, a bat squeak is a fantastic 200,000 vibrations a second. Higher frequency makes the sound higher, which is why bats squeak rather than growl. By the way, frequency is measured in hertz, (pronounced hurts and written Hz). So higher frequency makes more hertz.

Tuneful TONES

No, this has nothing to do with keeping in tone by physical exercise. A tone is a sound with just one frequency (just to confuse you, most sounds have lots all

9

mixed up). You can make a tone by hitting a special tool called a tuning fork on a smooth surface.

Rumbling RESONANCE (rez-o-nance)

This is when vibrations hit an object at a certain frequency. These make the object wobble too. The vibrations get stronger and stronger and the sound gets louder and louder. Until it can sound really deafening. (See page 28 for more details.)

Happenin' HARMONICS

All sounds are made up of harmonics. As long as the harmonics are working on the same frequency, things sound OK and keep your music teacher happy. If not, you're left with a *very* unpleasant noise. Harmonics are the basis of most music.

Got all that? That'll give you something to shout about in your next science lesson. But here's something you can make an even bigger noise about. Just imagine what it would be like if YOU became a real-life pop star...

Now's your chance...

Could you be a pop star?

You don't need too many qualifications to be a pop star. Although talent helps, it doesn't seem too vital. Just so long as you actually enjoy music and dancing YOU could be the latest hottest biggest new pop sensation. But you'll need to be ready to record your first hit single. To find out how, read on.

To show us the technical side of the business we've hired (at great expense) top DJ and record producer Jez Liznin. And to help explain the vital background facts about sound that any budding pop star needs to know we've recruited scientist, Wanda Wye.

Could you be a pop star? Step one: Sound systems
Silent soundproofing

When you record a hit record you don't want to pick up the sound of next door's TV. Jez's sound studio is lined with a thick hi-tech sound insulator to keep out unwanted noises.

OK, it's only cardboard egg boxes behind plasterboard.

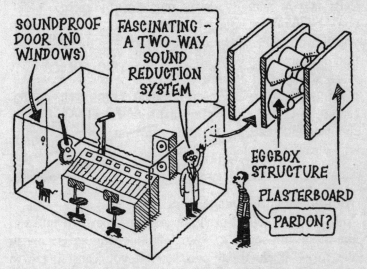

The soft cardboard soaks up the vibes like a nice comfy pillow. And they get lost in there, which is why it's so quiet in the studio. Except when Jez opens his big mouth.

Mighty microphone
This is what you'll need to sing or play instruments into. You'll need to get quite close to it, so you can call it mike for short.

What Wanda means is that the microphone turns sound into electric pulses. Like this…

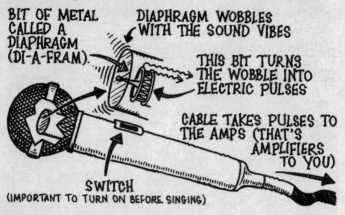

BIT OF METAL CALLED A DIAPHRAGM (DI-A-FRAM).

DIAPHRAGM WOBBLES WITH THE SOUND VIBES

THIS BIT TURNS THE WOBBLE INTO ELECTRIC PULSES

CABLE TAKES PULSES TO THE AMPS (THAT'S AMPLIFIERS TO YOU)

SWITCH (IMPORTANT TO TURN ON BEFORE SINGING)

Amplifiers and loudspeakers

Your mike would be pretty useless on its own. Thanks to the mike, the sound of your fabulous singing is now in the form of electrical pulses. And you can't listen to pulses, can you? Well, you could but it would be about as thrilling as listening to a hair dryer. So you need a loudspeaker to turn the pulses back into your own groovy tune. And an amplifier makes your tune loud enough to hear – sometimes a bit too loud.

YEAH, THEY'RE GIVING ME GREAT VIBES

AND THEY'RE GIVING ME A HEADACHE

LOUDSPEAKER

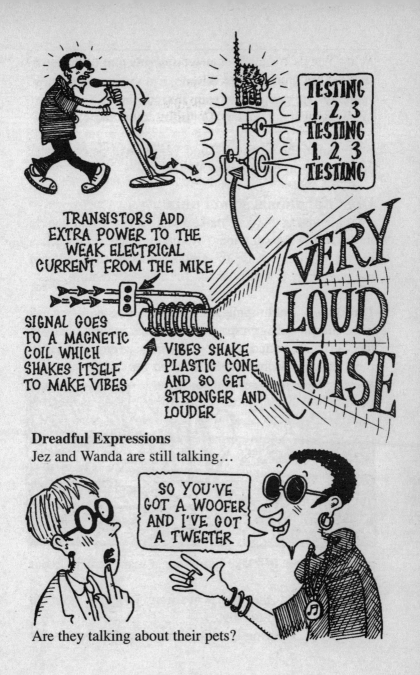

TRANSISTORS ADD EXTRA POWER TO THE WEAK ELECTRICAL CURRENT FROM THE MIKE

SIGNAL GOES TO A MAGNETIC COIL WHICH SHAKES ITSELF TO MAKE VIBES

VIBES SHAKE PLASTIC CONE AND SO GET STRONGER AND LOUDER

VERY LOUD NOISE

TESTING 1, 2, 3 TESTING 1, 2, 3 TESTING

Dreadful Expressions

Jez and Wanda are still talking…

SO YOU'VE GOT A WOOFER AND I'VE GOT A TWEETER

Are they talking about their pets?

Still want to be a star? Jez and Wanda will be back later on to give you more sound advice.

Dreadful animal sound quiz

Imagine that you are a small animal. What would you do in the following situations? Remember, your choice is a matter of life and death. Choose incorrectly and you might end up as a tasty snack for a larger creature.

1 You are a South American possum (poss-um – a small furry animal with a grasping tail that lives in trees) and you meet a Brazilian screaming frog. The frog screams (that's how it got its name, oddly enough). What do you do?

a) Eat the frog. It'll take more than a scary scream to put you off.
b) Run away – the frog is warning you that there's a dangerous animal nearby.
c) Back off. The frog is telling you it's poisonous to eat.

16

2 You're a North American ground squirrel. There's a rattlesnake in your burrow and it's after your babies. You can't see the snake but you can hear its sinister rattle. It sounds surprisingly high-pitched and slow. What do you do?

a) Run for it. The rattle warns you that the snake is big and poisonous. Yikes! The babies can fend for themselves.

b) The slow rattle means the snake is moving slowly. So you've got time to dig an escape tunnel for yourself and your babies.

c) Attack the snake. The rattle proves the snake is smaller than average and rather tired. So you might just win the fight.

3 You're a lapwing (a bird) living in a swamp. You hear a loud three-note call from a red shank (that's another type of bird). What do you do?

a) Go looking for fish. The cry tells you there's food nearby.

b) The call is a warning. There's a gang of crows in the way and they'd like to eat your babies (and the red shank's). You join a posse of other lapwings to fight the invaders off.
c) Nothing. The cry tells you rain's on the way and being a swamp bird you're not scared of a drop of water.

Bet you never knew!
Human beings also use sounds to communicate – so you knew that already? Well, bet you never knew that human voices can make more different sounds than any other mammal. That's because you can move your tongue and lips in many different ways to form lots of weird and wonderful sounds. Try making a few now...

Dare you discover… sounds all around you?

What you need:

Yourself

One pair of ears (If you're lucky you may already have these. You should find them attached to the sides of your head.)

What to do:

1 Nothing

2 Sit very still and listen.

What did you notice?

a) Nothing. And it gets really boring after the first half hour.

b) I started hearing all kinds of sounds I hadn't noticed before.

c) I heard strange sounds from inside my body.

Answer: b) and possibly **c)**. Sounds are all around us. There are loads of everyday sounds that we don't take any notice of. Sounds like the neighbour's cat throwing up fur balls, your gran sucking a wine gum, or a sparrow with a bad cough. If there aren't any sounds going on, you can always listen to your own breathing. (If you're not breathing it might be a good idea to see a doctor.)

Sounds dreadful fact file

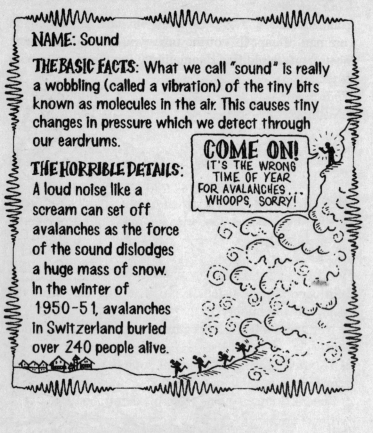

NAME: Sound

THE BASIC FACTS: What we call "sound" is really a wobbling (called a vibration) of the tiny bits known as molecules in the air. This causes tiny changes in pressure which we detect through our eardrums.

THE HORRIBLE DETAILS: A loud noise like a scream can set off avalanches as the force of the sound dislodges a huge mass of snow. In the winter of 1950–51, avalanches in Switzerland buried over 240 people alive.

COME ON! IT'S THE WRONG TIME OF YEAR FOR AVALANCHES... WHOOPS, SORRY!

COME OVER 'EAR AND WE'LL READ THE NEXT CHAPTER

DREADFUL  HEARING

Bats, humans and grasshoppers all have something in common. Ears. Most of the time you don't notice them. Well, not unless there's something dreadfully odd about them...

WHAT'RE YOU STARING AT?

But you'd soon notice if your own ears weren't working too well, and you'd certainly notice if you couldn't hear because behind your ears lies an amazing bit of natural engineering. Listen up.

Dreadful expressions

Two doctors are at the theatre. But can they hear the play?

AAAAARGH!

WELL, MY AUDITORY OSSICLES ARE AGITATING MY OVAL WINDOWS

Is this painful?

Answer: Not usually. She means the bones in her ear have vibrated and passed on their motion to the "oval window" covering the entrance to her inner ear. So her answer could have been, "Yes". Confused yet? Just lend an ear to this.

How sounds get into your head

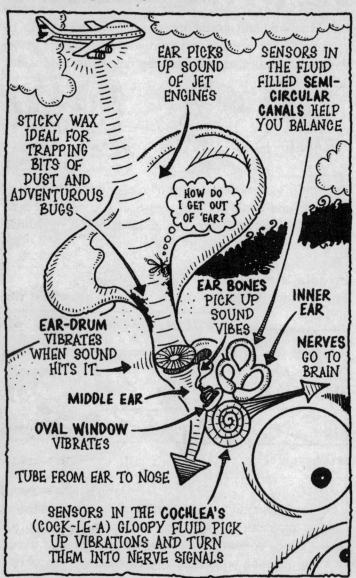

And here's the ear in action...

Imagine a wandering ugly bug, say a fly, sneaked into the ear. Here's what it would see.

1 The external ear canal (that's ear 'ole to you)

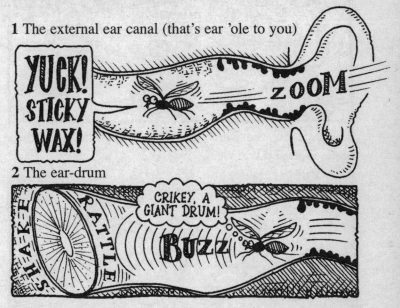

2 The ear-drum

3 Meanwhile, in the middle ear the ear bones are doing their castanets impression by passing on the fly's irritating buzz.

Can you see where the names came from?

4 The semi-circular canals

Scientists use the word "canal" to mean any long thin space in the body.

5 Cochlea

That fly's a genius. That's where the name comes from.

6 And the nerves are buzzing with sound messages for the brain.

Could you be a scientist?

Would you make a good sound scientist? Try to predict the results of these sound experiments. If you get them right you'll certainly have something to shout about.

1 Scientists have discovered that our hearing is sharpest for sounds of a certain frequency. Which sounds do we hear most clearly?

a) Loud music

b) A coin dropping on the floor

c) A teacher talking

2 Every musical instrument sounds a bit different even when they play the same note. Some make a smooth tinkling noise and some make more of a rattle or a blare. This is because of the unique pattern of sound vibrations or timbre (tim-bruh) made by each instrument. Scientist

25

Steve McAdams wanted to discover if people could spot these differences. What did he find?

a) People are useless at spotting sound differences. They said all the instruments sounded the same to them.

b) People are brilliant at this. They could tell the difference between the instruments even when Steve used a computer to take out almost all the timbre differences.

c) The experiments had to be stopped when the volunteers developed raging earache.

3 A scientist at Harvard Medical School, USA, studied electrical signals in the brain triggered by sounds. What do you think he found?

a) Tuneful sounds trigger wild signals in the brain.

b) All sounds trigger regular patterns of signals.

c) Tuneful sounds trigger regular patterns and dreadful clashing noises trigger wild signals.

Bet you never knew!
Diana Deutsch, Professor of Psychology at the University of California, USA, studied the way our ears hear different notes. She played different notes in each ear of a volunteer.

Amazingly, even when she played a high note in the left ear the volunteer said they heard the sound in their right ear. The experiment showed that your right ear "wants" to hear higher notes than the left ear. Sounds weird, doesn't it?

Horribly hard of hearing

But, of course, these sound experiments depend on one vital factor. Hearing. The volunteer had to hear the sounds in the first place, and some people can't.

Sounds dreadful fact file

NAME: Deafness

THE BASIC FACTS: About 16 per cent of people in Britain have less than perfect hearing. About one in twenty people have some difficulty in hearing conversation.

THE DREADFUL DETAILS:

1 Deafness can be caused by listening to loud music. This can destroy the nerve endings that join on to the cochlea. Better shout that to your noisy teenage brother or sister.

2 Disease can destroy hearing. Temporary deafness can occur when the middle ear gets infected and fills up with pus. Yuck!

3 As people get older the sensors in the cochlea die off. That's why you may have to shout in your gran's ear hole.

THANKS FOR THE NEW PYJAMAS, GRAN!

GO TO THE BAHAMAS? LOVELY, I'LL GO AND PACK!

Helpful hearing aids

Nowadays deafness can be helped by hearing-aids or cochlea implants. A hearing-aid is a miniature microphone linked to an amplifier that makes sounds louder. A cochlea implant is a tiny radio receiver fitted under the skin that receives radio signals from an earpiece behind the ear. The implant then converts the signals to electrical pulses that trigger signals along the nerves to the brain. Brilliant, eh?

Bet you never knew!
In the USA, a man named Henry Koch complained of hearing music in his head. Tests showed that a tiny lump of carborundum (car-bor-run-dum), a hard black chemical from a dentist's drill, had stuck in his tooth. The crystals in the chemical were picking up and boosting the power of radio waves from a nearby transmitter. This triggered vibrations which the poor man heard as music.

But before the invention of modern hearing aids, in about 1900, people had to make do with this...

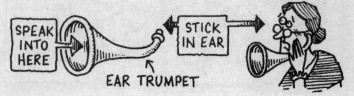

EAR TRUMPET

You shout into the ear trumpet. The vibrations can't escape from the trumpet except by passing into granny's lug hole. So your voice sounds louder.

But how would deafness affect a composer of music? A person for whom hearing is more important than anything else in the world. Someone like German composer Ludwig van Beethoven (1770-1827) for example.

Hearing is believing

Some people called him a genius. Others called him crazy and sometimes even ruder things. His music was inspired by listening to country sounds, murmuring streams, storms and bird calls. He composed thrilling, dramatic melodies that mirrored his passionate feelings about life and art. Hearing had made him what he was.

But in 1800 Beethoven noticed a ringing in his ears and over the next twenty years his hearing failed. He was forced to try a weird variety of different-shaped ear trumpets. The deafness might have been caused by a disease of the bones in Beethoven's middle ear.

The treatments he took were useless:

• Cold baths in smelly river water.

• Pouring almond oil into his ear holes.

• Wearing strips of bark over his ears.

• Wearing painful plasters on his arms until he got blisters.

Beethoven couldn't hear people talking. Instead, he wrote his friends little notes and they wrote back to him.

He gave his nephew Karl piano lessons and boasted the boy was brilliant. (He must be, thought Beethoven, because he had the best teacher in the world.) It was lucky Beethoven couldn't hear the young boy's dreadful playing. Beethoven's deafness made him really miserable. He also began to pong because he rarely bothered to wash or change his clothes. He never brushed his hair. (Don't get any ideas from this – missing a bath doesn't make you a genius.)

Beethoven could no longer hear well enough to conduct his own music. Several concerts were dreadful flops because he conducted the orchestra too slowly.

But amazingly enough, deafness didn't harm Beethoven's work as a composer. Some experts think he even got better. He used to imagine how the music would sound. And he had a special trick that helped him "listen" to a piano.

Dare you discover ... how to "hear" like Beethoven?

What you need:
One 0.5 cm (0.2 inch) wide rubber band
One pair of teeth – preferably your own

WARNING DON'T LET GO OF RUBBER BAND, SUDDENLY!

What you do:
1 Stretch the rubber band between your fingers and twang it. Note how loud the sound is.
2 Put one end of the band between your teeth. Stretch the band. (Don't let go!) Twang it again.

What did you notice?
a) The twang sounded louder the first time.
b) The twang sounded louder the second time.
c) The twang sounded a higher note the second time.

Answer: b) The twang sounds louder because the sound vibrations pass directly to your inner ear via the bones in your skull. These are very good at passing on sound vibrations. Beethoven used a drumstick held in his teeth to feel sound vibrations from a piano in the same way.

33

But for some people life is even harder. Try to imagine what it's like to be completely blind and deaf. The world would be dark and silent. And if you were a baby how would you ever learn a thing? This was the challenge for Helen Keller (1880-1968) who was deaf and blind and didn't know how to talk. Here's how her teacher, Annie O'Sullivan might have told her story...

A touch of magic
Boston, USA Spring 1927
The young reporter was in a hurry. He had a deadline to meet and the editor back at *The Daily Globe* office was getting impatient for his story.

"So, Annie, may I call you that? You were Helen's teacher for many years. But what was she really like?"

The old woman smiled weakly. "Well, she was very naughty when she was a young girl. She smashed her mum's plates and stuck her fingers in her dad's food. Then she'd pinch her grandma and chase her from the room."

The reporter raised an eyebrow and stopped scribbling in his notebook.

"So, the famous Helen Keller was a bit of a wild child? Our readers will be shocked."

"Helen couldn't hear or see after an illness that she'd had as a baby. She knew people talked using their lips and she wanted to join in. But she couldn't because she'd never learnt how to talk. So Helen got cross instead. She drove her parents crazy. Her uncle said she ought to be locked up somewhere."

The old woman took a sip of tea.

"So I bet Helen's parents were pleased when you turned up. You being a teacher of deaf children."

"Yes, they were! They'd written to my boss at the charity in desperation asking him to send someone and I got the job. But Helen was less impressed. I remember our first meeting like it was yesterday. I tried to give her a hug and she struggled like a wild cat."

The reporter tucked his pencil behind his ear.

"So the famous Helen Keller was like a wild cat," he smirked, "Bet you gave her a smack to keep her in line." The old lady looked shocked. Her saucer rattled as she replaced her cup.

"Oh no, that was never my way. I wanted Helen to be my friend as well as my pupil. Of course, I had to be firm sometimes..."

"Yeah, yeah," broke in the reporter, "but what our readers really want to know is how you taught her. I mean, it's not like she could hear or see anything."

"That was the big problem. All day long I tried to get Helen to understand me by tapping her hand. It was a special code – each letter of the alphabet was a certain number of taps. But Helen didn't understand. It was *so* frustrating."

"Don't suppose it meant anything to her seeing as she didn't know how to read or even what an alphabet was."

"Well, yes I know, but at the time I thought Helen would guess someone was trying to make contact. She'd already made up a few signs herself. Like when she wanted ice-cream she'd pretend to shiver."

The reporter was drumming his fingers and fidgeting. "OK, Annie. So you had a problem. How did you get through to Helen in the end?"

"Don't be so fast, young man, I was coming to that. One day we were out for a walk and came across a woman pumping water. Well, I had a brainwave. I put

Helen's hand under the stream, and I spelt out W-A-T-E-R by tapping on her hand. Helen twigged at once and then I knew what to do. I got Helen to feel or taste or smell things. For example, she learnt about the sea by paddling in the waves. Then I told her what they were by tapping. Yes, just like you're doing with your fingers."

The reporter stopped tapping as Annie continued...

"For Helen it was incredible, unbelievable. Just imagine it! You're locked in a totally dark and silent world for seven years, and then suddenly one day you realize that someone is actually trying to make contact with you. Helen changed as if by magic. She stopped being naughty and worked really hard."

The journalist checked his watch. Time was running short. He needed to spice up the story. A new angle.

"But Helen can talk now. What our readers want to know is how you managed to teach her."

"Helen knew things vibrate to make a sound. She could feel my throat move when I talked." Annie put her worn old fingers up to her thin neck. "We brought in a speech expert, Miss Fuller. By touching the teacher's throat and tongue and lips Helen found how they moved. Then she had a go herself.

"The first words Helen ever said were, 'I feel warm'. Well, she needed ten lessons just to get that far. But Helen stuck at it. And then..."

"You two went all over the world," interrupted the reporter as he buttoned his coat, "and Helen made grand speeches about the needs of people who can't see and hear." "Yes," the old lady agreed, "and we still live together. Thank goodness for our housekeeper Polly, she looks after Helen most of the time now as I'm getting on a bit. Matter of fact, they're both out in town shopping at the moment."

The reporter stifled a yawn as the old lady continued.

"Mind you, Helen is very capable – despite everything. As I'm sure you've heard, Helen went to university and got a degree. It was all her own work, you know."

The reporter chewed his pencil impatiently. Then he gave a nasty little smile. He scented the new angle.

"It's an amazing story, Annie. But our readers have heard it all before. Devoted teacher helps little girl to discover the world. But maybe there's another side. What do you say to people who claim Helen wasn't that smart and you did the work for her?"

The old lady looked at the young man blankly, then her face filled with anger.

"Well, that's where you're wrong!" she declared fiercely. "It was Helen who did the learning. Yes, Helen is clever – but that's not the point! You see, I'm blind now myself. Never could see much, in fact. But I've come to realize that even if they can't see or hear, quite ordinary people can still do amazing things. Helen Keller

38

taught me that."

The reporter felt stunned, but his mind was still fixed on the story. "Ordinary people can do amazing things..." *Hmm, I like that*, he thought as he closed his notebook. It would make a great opening line.

So that's hearing for you – tiny little air vibrations that rattle your ear bones. Sound waves seem pretty harmless, don't they? Well no, actually sound waves can be dreadful. They can smash windows and buildings and shake an entire aeroplane into little pieces. Now we're in for a bumpy ride, so fasten your seat belts and prepare for a bit of TURBULENCE.

Let's have a nice big round of applause for this chapter. Notice anything? When you clap your hands, the noise you hear is a sound wave. Sound waves are happening all around you all the time.

They zoom outwards like the ripples on a pond when you chuck a rock into the middle. But not all sound waves are the same...

Sounds dreadful fact file

NAME: Sound waves

THE BASIC FACTS: A sound wave happens when tiny air molecules are shoved together and bump apart again. As they leap apart some molecules bump into others further away.

So you get a wave of bumpy molecules moving outwards like the ripples on that pond.

THE DREADFUL DETAILS: It's not safe to stand next to a big bell when it rings. Powerful sound waves from the huge bell at Notre Dame Cathedral in Paris can burst blood vessels in your nose. Some visitors get nasty nose bleeds.

CLANG!

NEED A TISSUE?

Scientists use an amazing machine called an oscilloscope (o-sill-oscope) to measure sound waves. The sound waves make a beam of electrons (tiny high energy bits) jump about on a screen.

Here's what a sound wave looks like…

ISN'T THAT JUST BEAUTIFUL

A sound wave shows up as a curve or zigzag. The bigger the peak the greater the amplitude (loudness).

SUPER!

faster vibrations =
closer together peaks =
higher frequency =
higher pitch of sound

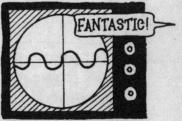

FANTASTIC!

Slower vibrations =
peaks further apart =
lower frequency =
lower pitch of sound

Fantastic frequency

Frequency is measured in Hertz (Hz) – that's vibrations per second, remember (see page 9). Your amazingly alert ears can pick up low-frequency sounds from about 25 vibrations per second, and they hear up to an ear-smacking 20,000 vibrations every second!

High-frequency sounds include...
• A mouse squeaking.

• A human squeaking after seeing the mouse.

• A bike chain in need of a drop of oil.

Low-frequency sounds include…
• A bear growling.

• Your dad growling in the morning.

• Your stomach growling before lunch.

Bet you never knew!
Small things vibrate faster. That's why they make higher frequency sounds than big things. So that's why your voice sounds higher than your dad's, and a violin sounds more squeaky than a double bass.

As you grow up, the vocal chords in your throat that make sounds get bigger. So your voice gets deeper.

Dare you discover ... how to see sound waves?

What you need:

A torch
A large piece of cling film
A cake tin without a base
A large elastic band
Sellotape
A piece of kitchen foil

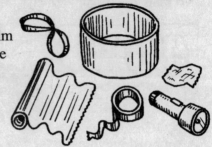

What you do:

1 Stretch the clingfilm tightly over one end of the cake tin. Secure the clingfilm using the elastic band as shown.
2 Use the sellotape to stick the piece of foil off-centre on the clingfilm as shown.

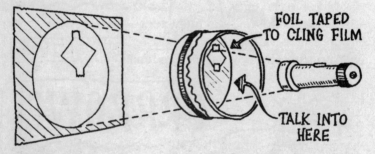

FOIL TAPED TO CLING FILM

TALK INTO HERE

3 Darken the room.
4 Place the torch on a table and angle it so the light reflects from the piece of foil on to the wall.
5 Talk into the open end of the cake tin.

What do you notice about the reflection?
a) It jumps around.
b) It stays rock steady.
c) The reflection gets brighter or dimmer depending on how loud your voice is.

Test your teacher

Here's your chance to sound your teacher out. Ask your teacher to say whether they think each answer is TRUE or FALSE, and here comes the tricky bit – ask them to explain *why*.

Important note: there are two marks for each correct answer. But your teacher is only allowed one mark if they only get the TRUE/FALSE bit right.

1 You can listen to a concert underwater even if you're at the other end of the swimming pool. TRUE/FALSE

2 You can use sound to count the number of times a fly flaps its wings in a second. TRUE/FALSE

3 You can hear sounds more quickly on a hot day. TRUE/FALSE

4 If you lived in a lead box you wouldn't be able to hear any sounds from the outside. TRUE/FALSE

Answers: 1 TRUE. Sound travels easily through water. That's why you can hear a rubber band twang even when you hold it underwater. Sound waves pass through water molecules in the same way as air molecules. But the concert would sound muffled because the water would press into your ears and stop your eardrums vibrating normally. (You could make this a trick question and say FALSE because no one can hold their breath that long.) 2 TRUE. Scientists know the number of vibrations per second for each musical note. All they have to do is to find a note that sounds the same as the beating of a fly's wing. The wing will beat at the same speed. Using this technique scientists have found that a housefly's wings beat 352 times a second. 3 TRUE. When air is warmer the molecules have more energy and move faster. But sound only travels about 3 per cent faster so you probably won't notice the difference. 4 FALSE. Sound passes easily through solid metal. But it does pass more slowly through lead compared with steel – 4,319 km per hour (2,684 mph), compared to 18,111 km per hour (11,254 mph). But you can still hear the sound clearly.

What your teacher's score means…
Score 7-8 points. This means EITHER
a) Your teacher is a genius. He/she is wasted as a teacher. We're dealing with Nobel Prize winning material here. OR
b) (More likely) they've read this book. In which case disqualify them for cheating.
Score 5-6 points. Fair but could do better. About average for a teacher.

Could you be a scientist?

One of the most amazing sound effects was discovered by an Austrian scientist called Christian Doppler (1803-1853). But in 1835 young Christian was desperate, dejected and departing. He couldn't find a job. So he sold all his belongings and got ready to set off for America.

At the last minute, a letter arrived offering him a job as Professor of Mathematics at Prague University (now in the Czech Republic). This was a stroke of luck because it was here that Doppler discovered what became known as the Doppler effect.

Doppler reckoned that when a moving sound passes it always changes pitch in the same way – that's the Doppler effect. As the sound waves come towards you they're squashed together. So you hear them in quick succession at a higher frequency. As the sound moves away you hear it at a lower frequency because the sound waves are more widely spaced.

To test Doppler's weird idea a Dutch scientist called Christoph Buys Ballot (1817-1890) filled a train carriage with buglers and listened as they whizzed past him. What do you think he heard?

Clue: the test proved Doppler was right.

a) As the buglers came closer the sound grew higher. As they moved away the sound got lower.

b) As the buglers came closer the sound grew lower. As they moved away the sound got higher.

c) The buglers were out of tune and the roar of the train almost drowned them out.

Answer:
a) Higher frequency sound waves = higher sounds, remember? If you stand by a busy road and listen to cars going past you can hear the Doppler effect for yourself. Award yourself half a mark if your answer was **c)**. These problems did happen but not badly enough to spoil the experiment.

Supersonic sound scientists

Have you ever watched a distant firework display? Ever wondered why you see the lovely coloured sparks but don't hear the bangs until a moment or two later?

It proves light travels faster than sound. But how fast does sound travel? A French priest called Marin Mersenne (1588-1648) had a brilliant plan to check it out.

He got a friend to fire a cannon. Marin stood a distance away and timed the gap between the flash when the gun was fired and the bang when the sound waves reached him.

But he didn't have an accurate clock so he counted his heartbeats instead.

In fact, he didn't do too badly. After scientists measured the speed of sound accurately they realized Marin's figure, 450 metres (1,480 feet) per second was a bit fast. But maybe Marin got excited and his heart speeded up.

One cold day in 1788, two French scientists fired two cannon 18 km (11.3 miles) apart. The second cannon provided a double check on the first and the distance between the two was about as far as each scientist could see with a telescope. They counted the time between the flashes and the bangs.

But what scientists really needed was a bit of posh equipment to make a more accurate measurement. And that's why French scientist Henri Regnault (1810-1878) built this ingenious sound machine. But would it work – or was it just a long shot?

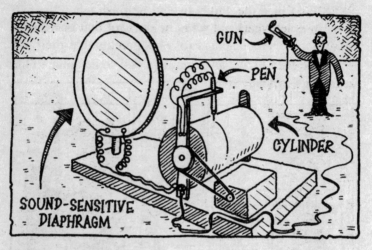

Here's what happened...
1 The cylinder went round at a regular speed and the pen made a line.
2 The pen was controlled by two electric circuits.
3 When the gun fired the circuit was broken and the pen-line jumped to a new position. I suppose that's what you call "jumping the gun". Ha, ha!
4 When the diaphragm picked up the sound, the circuit was restored and the pen flicked back to its original position.
Regnault knew how fast the cylinder was turning. So he measured the marks made by the pen and this told him how quickly the test had happened. His measurements proved sound travels at 1,220 km/h (760 mph).

But despite Regnault's hard work the measure for the speed of sound is named after a completely different scientist.

Hall of fame: Ernst Mach (1835-1916),
Nationality: Austrian

Ernst was ten years old when he decided that his lessons were boring. His teachers told his parents that their son was "stupid".

WOODLICE HAVE BIGGER BRAINS

"So a teacher called him stupid – what's new?" I hear you say. Well, instead of giving young Ernst a hard time his mum and dad took him away from school and he grew up to be a scientific genius. It might be worth trying this story on your parents – but I doubt it will work.

Ernst's dad bred silkworm caterpillars to make silk and was also very keen on science. His mum loved art and poetry, and between them they taught young Ernst at home. The boy learnt his lessons in the morning and in the afternoon he helped with the silkworms.

At 15 Ernst went back to school where science became his favourite subject. He went on to teach science at university, but he was so poor that he decided to study the science of hearing for which he wouldn't need to buy expensive equipment. His own ears would do fine.

In 1887 Ernst was studying missiles that flew faster than sound waves. He found that at supersonic speeds (that means faster than sound) the wave of air pushed out in front of the missile changes direction.

This allowed the missile to travel smoothly at a supersonic speed.

By 1929 some scientists were dreaming of aeroplanes that could fly faster than sound. So they decided to honour Ernst's discovery by measuring speed in Mach numbers (Mach 1 was the speed of sound). But the scientists faced a dreadful problem. It seemed no human could ever travel that fast ... and live.

The cone of death

Although, as Mach showed, a missile could fly at speeds faster than sound, there was a lot of bumpiness on the way. As a flying object nears the speed of sound the air forming the sound waves can't escape fast enough. The air piles up around the plane in a massive invisible cone. A cone of death. The shaking and buffeting of the air cone was enough to tear an ordinary plane to pieces.

I'M SHAKING AND OUT OF CONTROL, OVER ...

IT'S JUST NERVES - YOU HAVEN'T TAKEN OFF YET

By 1947 every pilot who had flown near the speed of sound had been killed. Pilots called it "the sound barrier".

But in a secret airfield in California, USA, one young man dreamed of breaking through the barrier in a specially strengthened plane that was designed for high-speed flight. Would tragedy strike again? If one of the project's engineers had kept a secret diary it might have read something like this:

THE SECRET DIARY OF CHUCK YEAGER'S ENGINEER

12 October 1947

Morning

Poor Chuck. What a disaster! He's only fallen off a horse. Bust three ribs - now he can't even move his right arm. I really sympathize with Chuck, but it looks like he's out of the running for the sound barrier attempt. He can't fly a super-fast X-1 plane with only one hand, can he?

Chuck looks really miserable. He can be very determined when he wants.

"I've been training for months. Eight flights so far - each time a bit faster and this is the big one. It'll take more than a few bust ribs to stop me." he snaps at me.

There's an icy feeling in the pit of my stomach. I think to myself, THIS IS CRAZY.

But I know he'll try it anyway, so I figure I'd better help.

Ooo... ← me

Afternoon

The main trouble with Chuck's injuries is that he can't reach far enough to close the X-1's door with his left hand. I poke around in the hanger and find a broomstick. I cut it to size and Chuck manages to close the door using the stick. Don't know how it'll work at 20,000 feet though.

14 October
8.00 am

We're just taking off from the bomber base. The X-1

LIKE THIS

is slung under the plane we're in. Chuck seems very calm but I can see from his face he's in a lot of pain. "I'm all right," he grimaces. "But I keep thinking about all the pilots who have been killed trying to break the barrier." Well, if that doesn't put him off what will? I wish I could think of something.

R.I.P.

A few minutes later....
This is it. Chuck's climbing down a ladder into the X-1. Now that I've said "Goodbye" to Chuck, I can't help wondering if I'll get a

chance to say "Hi, Chuck" again. My fingers are crossed.

Then I hear the click as the X-1's door locks smoothly. Three cheers for the broomstick handle! But if anything happens to Chuck... it'll be down to that piece of wood, and me. I helped him after all.

We can hear Chuck over the radio link with the X-1.

"Brrr, it's cold," he complains.

IT'S COLD!

Well, I'm not surprised, I think. There's hundreds of gallons of liquid oxygen fuel on that plane. It has to be stored at $-188°C$ $(-307°F)$. That's cold enough to frost over the windshield from the inside. Lucky we hit on the shampoo idea. That was a neat trick! Squirt a layer of shampoo on the glass and it stops the frost from forming.

10.50 am

"This is it," says the pilot of our plane nervously. He starts the countdown, "Five... four... three... two... one..."

My heart's in my mouth. Can Chuck really fly the X-1 with just one hand? Should I have stopped him?

"DROP!"

WHOOSH

Too late now he's on his way.

Chuck's got seconds to flick the ignition switch and start the X-1's engines. But if there's a spark near the fuel, the X-1 will be blown to bits. But the engine's firing perfectly. There she goes! Phew!

"I'm beginning to run," yells Chuck.

But we can't cheer yet.

He's hitting turbulence. Here comes the sound barrier – the next few moments are critical. Will the X-1 fall to pieces like the other planes? The seconds tick away... We hear only silence.

There's a sudden rumble. Is it thunder? No – it's the boom made as Chuck flies faster than sound. He's done it! The X-1's flying smoothly at Mach 1.05! HE'S BROKEN THE SOUND BARRIER! YES, YES, YES!!!

WHOOPEE!

BOOM

2.00 pm
Glad to be back on solid ground. I'm shattered. Chuck has a huge grin all over his face. He looks on top of the world so I ask him how he's feeling.

"Not so bad!" he laughs.

Not so bad. Not so bad for a guy with three busted ribs!

Booming marvellous sonic booms

Chuck Yeager had proved people can travel smoothly and safely at speeds faster than sound. And today jet planes like Concorde regularly break the sound barrier.

If this happens near you you'll hear all about it. Remember the sound like thunder made by Chuck's plane as it smashed through the sound barrier? You'll hear something similar. It'll rattle your windows, shake your chimney pots and possibly give your hamster a nervous breakdown. And the cause of this deadly force? Er – air. All those trillions of air molecules squashed together in front of the plane and fanning out behind it. When they hit the ground you hear this extraordinary sound. It's called a sonic boom.

Dare you discover ... how to hear a sonic boom?

Here's your chance to check out your very own sonic boom – otherwise known as a peal of thunder. Lightning is a searing hot spark caused by a build up of electricity in a storm cloud. This heats the surrounding air and makes a giant vibration that whizzes faster than sound. This makes the sonic boom we call thunder. Are you brave enough to probe its secrets?

RAIN, RAIN, RAIN, RAIN! WE NEED SOMETHING TO BRIGHTEN THINGS UP . . .

ARGH! FIRE! WE NEED MORE RAIN!

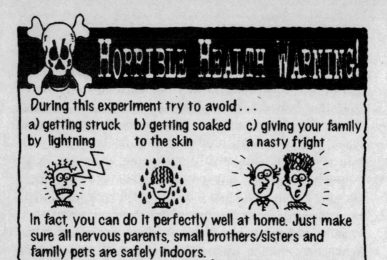
What you need:
A thunderstorm
Yourself
A watch with a second hand

What you do:
Watch the thunder and lightning.
1 *What do you notice?*
a) Thunder always comes before lightning.
b) Lightning always comes before thunder.
c) Thunder and lightning always happen at the same time.

Count the seconds between the lightning and the thunder.
2 *What do you notice?*
a) There's always the same time gap between the two.
b) The harder it rains the longer the gap becomes.
c) The time gap seems to get shorter or longer each time.

> **Answers: 1 b)** Light travels much faster than sound so you'll always see lightning before you hear thunder. **2 c)** You see lightning more or less instantly. As the storm moves towards you, the distance the thunder needs to travel gets shorter so you hear it sooner. As the storm moves away, the thunder takes longer to reach you. You can work out the position of the storm by counting the seconds between the lightning and the thunder. The sound of the thunder travels at 1 km in 3 seconds (1 mile in 5 seconds).

But if you think thunder's loud, there are noises in the next chapter that make thunder sound like a gnat burping! Get out your ear plugs (make sure they're clean, first!) and prepare to be SHATTERED!

SHATTERING SOUNDS

What's the loudest sound you've ever heard? Your little brother/sister bawling? Your grandad snoring? Or maybe you've heard something REALLY NOISY. Like a pop concert or a high speed train in a hurry. Here's a chart to compare the loudness of sounds.

TYPE OF NOISE	DECIBELS	EFFECT ON YOU →
You accidentally drop a sweet wrapper during a science lesson. WHOOPS!	10dB	So quiet no one notices. Phew! (Pick it up later)
You whisper to your friend during the lesson.	20-30dB	Sssh! People can hear you.
You start chatting to your friend. NATTER CHATTER!	60dB	Your teacher can hear you now. This could be painful.
The whole class starts chatting.	75dB	Ooh-er! Take cover!

Scientists measure the amplitude (loudness) of sound in bels and decibels (1 decibel=1 dB=10 bels). They're named after British-American inventor Alexander Graham Bell (1847-1922) (see page 105). By the way, just to confuse you, every time you go up three dB the sound gets about twice as loud. Got that? So 4 dB is roughly twice as loud as 1 dB.

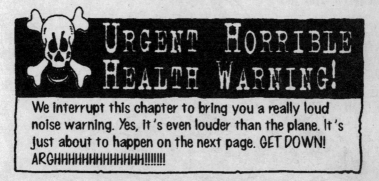

URGENT HORRIBLE HEALTH WARNING!

We interrupt this chapter to bring you a really loud noise warning. Yes, it's even louder than the plane. It's just about to happen on the next page. GET DOWN! ARGHHHHHHHHHHHHH!!!!!!!

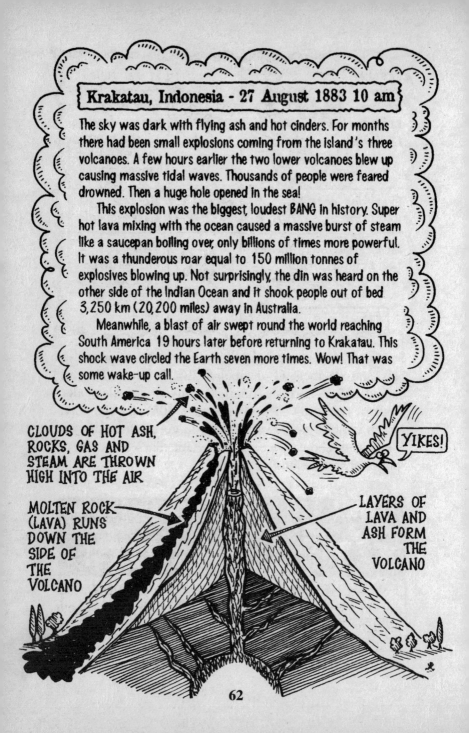

Krakatau, Indonesia - 27 August 1883 10 am

The sky was dark with flying ash and hot cinders. For months there had been small explosions coming from the island's three volcanoes. A few hours earlier the two lower volcanoes blew up causing massive tidal waves. Thousands of people were feared drowned. Then a huge hole opened in the sea!

This explosion was the biggest, loudest BANG in history. Super hot lava mixing with the ocean caused a massive burst of steam like a saucepan boiling over, only billions of times more powerful. It was a thunderous roar equal to 150 million tonnes of explosives blowing up. Not surprisingly, the din was heard on the other side of the Indian Ocean and it shook people out of bed 3,250 km (20,200 miles) away in Australia.

Meanwhile, a blast of air swept round the world reaching South America 19 hours later before returning to Krakatau. This shock wave circled the Earth seven more times. Wow! That was some wake-up call.

CLOUDS OF HOT ASH, ROCKS, GAS AND STEAM ARE THROWN HIGH INTO THE AIR

YIKES!

MOLTEN ROCK (LAVA) RUNS DOWN THE SIDE OF THE VOLCANO

LAYERS OF LAVA AND ASH FORM THE VOLCANO

Teacher's tea-time teaser

This terribly tasteless teatime teaser will set your teacher's teeth on edge. Tap quietly on the staff room door and when it groans open quietly ask:

I WAS JUST WONDERING WHY IT MAKES SUCH A HORRIBLE SCREECHING SOUND WHEN YOU SCRATCH YOUR FINGERNAILS DOWN THE BLACKBOARD?

GROAN!

Answer: Brr! Just thinking about it makes you shudder. The sound is made as the fingernail drags downwards. It touches rapidly on lots of tiny bumps on the surface of the board. This makes high frequency vibrations that you hear as the horrible noise. The vibrations are so uneven that they sound really tuneless and perhaps that's why they give you the shivers.

Noise nuisance

1 Are you being kept awake by noise? Maybe you've got noisy neighbours or a bawling baby brother or an anti-social parrot. Or maybe there's thundering traffic nearby? Cheer up, research shows you can sleep even when there's 40-60 dB of noise going on. If you're used to the noise, that is.

2 Nothing new about this. In ancient Rome, Julius Caesar passed a law to stop people driving noisy chariots about at night. They were keeping the citizens awake. But the chariot drivers didn't take any notice.

3 But louder noises are more of a headache – literally. Back in the 1930s, scientists found that factory workers worked harder when they wore ear-muffs to drown out noise. And people who worked in noisy places often felt bad-tempered after a hard day. (That's their excuse, anyway.)

4 Deafening noises can seriously damage your health. Scientists exposed to DREADFULLY LOUD sounds of 130 dB look a bit like this.

GIDDY →

130 dB

130 dB

SWOLLEN FINGER JOINTS

WOBBLING CHEST

NUMB HANDS AND FEET

5 In the 1970s, NASA scientists in the USA built a machine that made a racket registering 210 dB. (Fancy living next door to that?) The sound waves from this din were so powerful they could knock holes in solid objects.

6 In 1997 it was reported that US military bases in Britain were to be defended by powerful sound guns. Sound waves from these machines would make any intruder's intestines vibrate so much they'd need to find a toilet in a hurry. (Sounds dreadful!)

DON'T SUPPOSE YOU COULD LEND ME A CLEAN PAIR OF PANTS?

7 Scientists in France have developed an even deadlier weapon powered by an aircraft engine. It makes powerful infrasound waves – that's sounds too low for us to hear. But this sinister sound can make people feel sick and dizzy. The powerful sound vibrations shake the body's vital organs causing fatal damage. It can actually kill a person if they're less than 7 km (4 miles) away! Hopefully such a horrific machine will never be fired – but ordinary sound has already been used as...

A sound weapon

In 1989 US forces invaded Panama, in Central America in a bid to arrest the suspected drugs dealer General Manuel Noriega. But the wily General, (nick-named "old pineapple face") had fled his luxury villa for the Vatican embassy. The Americans were stumped. They couldn't gatecrash the embassy to grab the General. It was against international law. So "old pineapple face" was safe. Or was he?

Someone had a seriously sound idea. Why not blast the General out with sound? Here's what their notes to the General might have looked like (if they'd sent any)...

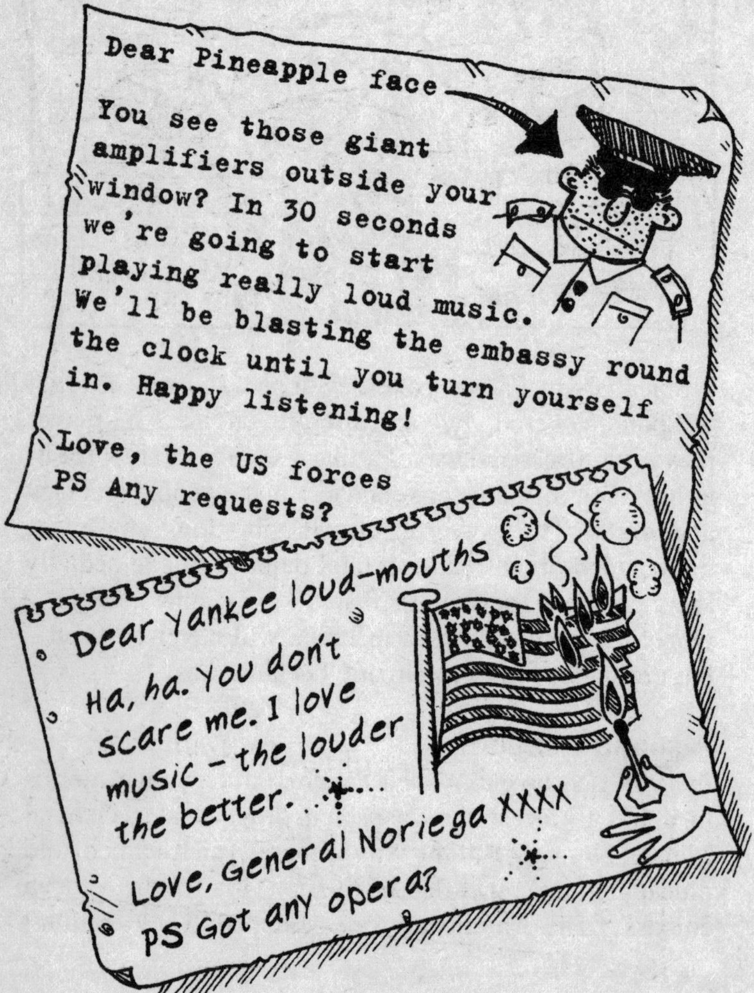

Dear Pineapple face

You see those giant amplifiers outside your window? In 30 seconds we're going to start playing really loud music. We'll be blasting the embassy round the clock until you turn yourself in. Happy listening!

Love, the US forces
PS Any requests?

Dear Yankee loud-mouths

Ha, ha. You don't scare me. I love music – the louder the better...

Love, General Noriega XXXX
PS Got any opera?

Dear Pineapple face

OK, you've had your classical music. Now for some really heavy rock! Yeah – it's time for something seriously LOUD by sixties guitar legend Jimi Hendrix.

Hope you like it!

Love, the US forces
PS Got the message yet?
PPS Come out with your hands up!
And this one's for you, General.

Dear No-good Yankees

Ow, my head hurts!
I can't stand it anymore.
I can't sleep, I can't think,
I can't eat. I'm going
crazy – I just can't take
it. OK, OK, you win. I surrender. Just
turn that dreadful noise down. Please!

Love, General Noriega
PS Got any headache pills?

Oh, so you like a bit of noise then? Really wild noise? Well, you'll lurve the next chapter. It's wild all right. Wild, woolly and hungry with huge bloodthirsty fangs. Are you wild enough to read on...? Howwwwwwwwl!

NOISY NATURE

Some people think that nature is quiet. Peaceful, tranquil, serene. But animals are never quiet. Their world is full of appalling growling, yowling, howling cries, and what's more they don't care if they keep you awake. Here's your chance to hear from some dreadfully loud wildlife.

The first ever

ANIMAL CONCERT

Live from the Heart of the Jungle

(Sponsored by Bert's Pet Shop)

THE CHOIR

The fantastic FROG male voice choir

CROAK! CROAK! CROAK!*

Delightful loud croaks made louder thanks to vibrating air-filled pouches in their throats. They'll be performing their romantic love song, *"Come here you lady frogs we'd lurve to meet you!"

The rowdy RATS

Famous for their squeaky songs. Some of them perform in ultrasound – that's notes too high-pitched for us to hear. They will be performing their traditional song of welcome to visiting rats,

SQUEAK! SQUEAK! SQUEAK! *

DON'T LIKE THE SOUND OF THIS MUCH

*"Clear off you dirty rats or we'll kill you!"
(The ultrasound version is a bit wasted on humans.)

QUACK! CUCKOO! TWITTER! CHIRRUP! CHIRP! OH DEAR!

The sensational SONG BIRDS

Hear them warble away with their amazing singing syrinxes (see-rinx-es) – that's the skin stretched over their windpipes. (It's the vibrations that make a whistling sound.)

(APOLOGY. The different types of birds are refusing to sing one song and insisting on singing their own tunes all at the same time. This may prove confusing.)

The high-flying HOWLER MONKEYS

HOWL!*

Performing their hit single, *"Get lost you other monkeys – this is our patch!" WARNING. These monkeys can be heard 15 km (9 miles) away. Members of the audience are respectfully advised to stick their fingers in their ears.

PANT HOO!
PANT HOO!
PANT HOO!
PANT HOO!

The charming cheeky CHIMPS

Will be performing their exciting new song, "Pant hoo, pant hoo, pant hoo." Roughly translated this means, "Come over here, there's some scrumptious fruit on this tree."

THE ORCHESTRA
(PERCUSSION SECTION)

The wild and wonderful WOODPECKERS

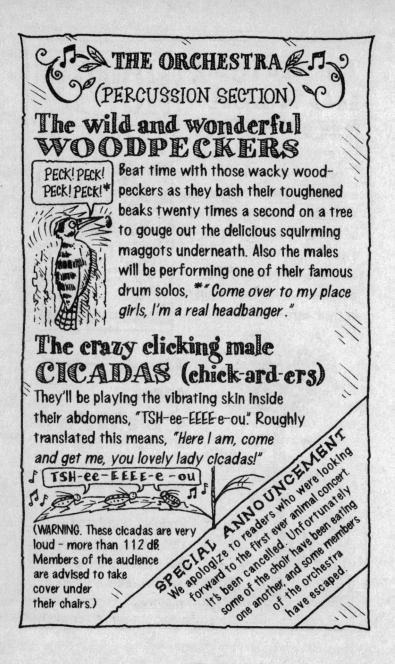

PECK! PECK! PECK! PECK!*

Beat time with those wacky woodpeckers as they bash their toughened beaks twenty times a second on a tree to gouge out the delicious squirming maggots underneath. Also the males will be performing one of their famous drum solos, *"Come over to my place girls, I'm a real headbanger."

The crazy clicking male CICADAS (chick-ard-ers)

They'll be playing the vibrating skin inside their abdomens, "TSH-ee-EEEE-e-ou." Roughly translated this means, "Here I am, come and get me, you lovely lady cicadas!"

♪ TSH-ee-EEEE-e-ou

(WARNING. These cicadas are very loud – more than 112 dB. Members of the audience are advised to take cover under their chairs.)

SPECIAL ANNOUNCEMENT

We apologize to readers who were looking forward to the first ever animal concert. It's been cancelled. Unfortunately some of the choir have been eating one another, and some members of the orchestra have escaped.

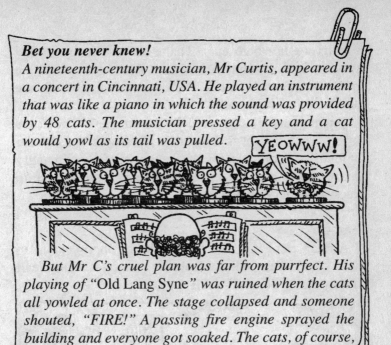

YEOWWW!

But Mr C's cruel plan was far from purrfect. His playing of "Old Lang Syne" was ruined when the cats all yowled at once. The stage collapsed and someone shouted, "FIRE!" A passing fire engine sprayed the building and everyone got soaked. The cats, of course, escaped by a whisker.

Hop it!

Have you ever heard a grasshopper stridulate (strid-u-late)? If you answered, "I often stride when late," then read on. Stridulating is the sound grasshoppers make by rubbing their hairy little legs together. (No, your pet gerbil can't do this – I don't care if he has got hairy little legs.) Male grasshoppers stridulate to serenade fanciable female grasshoppers.

But even when grasshoppers make a racket it's really hard to tell exactly where they're hiding. Scientists have found that the frequency of the noise is about 4,000 Hz, and it so happens that humans aren't very good at judging the direction of these sounds. Higher pitched sounds can be found using one ear, but for lower pitched sounds we use both ears. That's because longer sound waves bend around our heads. But with sounds in between we're a bit stuck. Well, we can't listen with one and a half ears can we?

Animals are a lot better at this hearing lark. They have to be. They've got to keep their ears open for smaller animals to scoff and for the heavy footfalls of hungry beasts out to scrunch them. Now 'ere's your chance to guess how good they are.

Ear, ear

1 African elephants (the ones with big floppy ears) can hear better than Indian elephants (the ones with small floppy ears). TRUE/FALSE

NICE HAT!

2 Some moths have ears on their wings. TRUE/FALSE

3 Crickets have ears on their legs. TRUE/FALSE

4 Snakes have ears hidden under their scales. TRUE/FALSE

5 Frogs have ears ... er, somewhere. TRUE/FALSE

6 An owl's face picks up sound like a large ear. TRUE/FALSE

7 Aardvarks have incredible hearing. They can hear termites scuttling about underground. TRUE/FALSE

8 Indian false vampire bats (I kid you not – that's what they're called) can hear tiptoeing mice. TRUE/FALSE

Answers: 1 FALSE. Larger ears don't help African elephants hear better but they do help keep them cool. Their big ears allow more blood to flow just under the skin and so lose body heat into the outside air. **2** TRUE. Lacewing moths have ears on their wings. All insect ears are thin flaps of skin that vibrate in response to sound just like your ear drums. The vibes trigger nerves to send messages to the insect's tiny little brain. **3** TRUE. Grasshoppers have ears on their abdomens, that's the rear part of their bodies. Crickets and grasshoppers make sound to attract a mate and use their ears to listen out for others of the same species (type of insect). **4** FALSE. Snakes don't have ears. They can't hear noises but they can sense the vibrations made by anything walking on the ground. Snakes pick up these signals through their jaw bones. **5** FALSE. Frogs don't have ears but they have ear drums on each side of their heads. Scientists have played different sounds to frogs. They found that frogs are best at picking up low frequency sounds – like croaks! **6** TRUE. An owl's face is shaped a bit like a satellite dish. It's brilliant at picking up sounds and bouncing them towards the owl's ear holes at the edge of the "dish". **7** TRUE. Then the aardvarks dig the termites up with their paws and lick them up with a long, sticky tongue. Tastee! **8** TRUE. The bats swoop down and grab the mice. But the mice do have a chance – they can hear the bat's high-pitched calls.

75

Chatting cetaceans

Cetaceans (see-tay-shuns) is the posh word for whales and dolphins. Use it in a science lesson and you're bound to make a big splash.

Some of the most amazing animal calls are made by dolphins and whales. They moo like cows, trill like birds, and whistle like ... er, whistles. They can even creak like a rusty old door hinge. All these sounds are made in rapid pulses of little more than a few milliseconds. But blue and fin whale calls can measure 188 dB. That's loud enough to damage your ears and be heard by other whales 850 km (530 miles) away.

We don't know what these sounds mean. They could be a way for the animals to keep in touch or chat to their friends. But some boring scientists have pointed out that cetaceans can make the sounds as soon as they're born. So they obviously don't learn a language like we do. They must learn something in a school of whales, though – ha ha!

Teacher's tea-time teaser

Tap gently on the staff room door and when it squeaks open smile sweetly and ask:

" 'SCUSE ME, I WAS JUST WONDERING HOW DOLPHINS AND WHALES SING UNDER WATER WITHOUT GETTING A MOUTHFUL OF OCEAN?"

SPLUTTER!

Answer: It's hard to sing underwater or to talk while you are slurping tea. But whales and dolphins can sing with their mouths shut. They make the sounds in a separate system of air passages linked to blowholes on top of their heads. (Scientists aren't sure exactly how the sounds are made.) Whales and dolphins can even sing underwater while chomping their breakfasts. Unlike you ... so **don't** try it.

Dolphins and killer whales also make other, even stranger sounds. They make weird ultrasound clicks. In the 1950s American scientists found that dolphins could find food at the bottom of a murky pool on a dark night. Tests showed the animals were making the clicks and then picking up the echoes from an object to find food.

Amazing things, echoes. Unearthly, ghostly sounds – scary voices without bodies, and by some eerie coincidence the next chapter's all about them.

LET'S GO!

EERIE ECHOES

Here's a treat if you like the sound of your own voice. Stand about 30 metres (98 feet) from a wall. Shout really loudly. Listen. Can you hear your own voice echoing from the wall? Sounds kind of eerie, doesn't it?

Eerie echo facts

1 An echo is made by sound waves bouncing off a surface in the same way as light bounces off a mirror.

2 So where's the best place to hear echoes? Well, why not try an eerie old castle? There's one near Milan, Italy, where you can hear your voice echoing over forty times. The old walls trap the sound waves so they continue bouncing backwards and forwards.

3 The domes of St Paul's Cathedral, London, and the Capitol building in Washington, USA, both feature eerie whispering galleries. You can whisper something against the walls and someone across the dome can hear your whispers. The curve of the walls directs the echoes to a single point on the other side. So if you want to whisper a joke about your teacher make sure they are safely out of the building.

SIR'S A BIT LIKE ST PAUL'S ...AN ANCIENT STRUCTURE WITH A SMOOTH DOME ON TOP

I'LL SEE YOU ON THE COACH, MISS WATKINS!

4 Alpine horns, the incredibly long horns that people play in Switzerland, use echoes to boost their range by several kilometres. The eerie echoes rumble around the mountains, and they can be used to send simple messages.

5 Fog horn echoes also have an eerie message. The low-pitched notes of the fog horn carry a long distance and any echoes will bounce off cliffs and rocks, warning of deadly danger ahead.
6 There's nothing more eerie than the booming rumble of thunder. Much of this sound is made by echoes rebounding off clouds from the original peal of thunder.
7 But there's more to echoes than noise. Music also requires echoes to come eerily alive...

Design your own concert hall
Well CONGRATULATIONS, your school has just been awarded a special grant to build a new concert hall, and you've been asked to lend a hand with the design. Got any ideas? It's important to plan the inside carefully so

people can hear music clearly. This is known as acoustics. Fortunately, we've got Jez Liznin to advise us.

1 The first thing we need is a big tank of water. You can make a ripple and watch it bounce from the walls of the tank.

A TANK HELPS TO PLAN THE WAY THAT SOUND WILL BOUNCE OFF THE WALLS OF THE HALL

2 Now let's look at the walls. Let's go for a curved wall around the back of the stage.

3 Avoid flat, smooth walls in your design. You'll get loads of echoes bouncing around in the wrong places – it'll be like being stuck in a tunnel.

4 Avoid comfy chairs and carpets and curtains. They'll soak up the sound and make the music sound rather dead. Hard chairs are better for the acoustics even if they do give you a sore bum.

5 Yes, that's right. You've got to build it. Didn't we tell you? Don't work too hard! Byeee!

Dreadful expressions

Should you call the police?

Could you be a scientist?

Scientists have been keen on bats for years. So is it true all scientists are seriously batty? In 1794, for example, Swiss scientist Charles Jurinne found that bats couldn't find their way around obstacles when they had their ears blocked.

But it wasn't until the 1930s that US scientist Donald R. Griffin recorded a bat's ultrasound squeaks and proved they found their way around in the dark by listening to the echoes. Can you imagine flying dolphins?

One of many batty experiments carried out by batty scientists involved trying to confuse bats by playing noise. What do you think happened?

a) The bats stopped flying and slumped to the ground.

b) The bats flew more slowly and made more noise themselves.

c) The bats beat the scientists with their leathery wings.

Answer: b) It takes more than a bit of noise to bother a bat. But the bats were put off a bit because they did fly more carefully than usual.

Bet you never knew!
Different types of bat squeak on different frequencies and amplitudes. For example, the little brown bat has a call as loud as a smoke detector. (No, don't get any ideas – it's cruel to use bats as safety equipment.) But the whispering bat has a call that's only as loud as … believe it or not … a whisper. But whatever they call it, any bat could mean dreadful danger – if you happen to be a moth.

THE TIGER MOTH SURVIVAL MANUAL

by Squadron Leader
Irma Tiger-Moth

> OK, AIR CREW, PAY ATTENTION TO THIS BRIEFING. IT COULD MEAN THE DIFFERENCE BETWEEN LIFE AND DEATH.

Here's your main enemy – a bat. Take a good look. Ugly looking blighter isn't he? Could be the last thing you see. So remember – Biting Bats Scoff Moths. They open their mouths wide and scrunch us with their sharp little fangs. What a terrible way to go! No wonder we moths are miffed.

a bat

MAKE SURE YOU LEARN THE FOLLOWING PROCEDURES BY HEART

1 Listen hard for bat squeaks. They mean there's a bat about, and it's flying your way! Luckily, you can

hear the bats before they
detect you so RUN FOR IT –
er, I mean FLY FOR IT!

SQUEAK

YIKES!

EH?

POP! POP!

2 If the bat gets too close
activate your vesicles.
These are those tiny ridge plates
on each side of your body, in
case you didn't know. Squeeze
'em hard and the ridges make a
loud pop noise. This'll confuse
the bat. Ha, ha – serves 'em right.

3 While the bat's working out what's going on – you
make your escape. It's best to drop to the ground. The
cowardly bat will be too scared of crashing to follow
you. Also, their echo sounders can't spot you on the
ground. That's because they get so many echoes from the
ground they can't make out which echoes are bouncing
off you.

PHEW!

I GIVE
UP!

Eventually, millions of years after bats and dolphins had the idea – humans decided to use echoes to find things. Or at least one brainy French scientist did.

Hall of fame: Paul Langevin (1872-1946)
Nationality: French

Young Paul was one of those kids who's always top of the class. He never came second in anything. Makes you sick, doesn't it? So I won't even tell you about how he taught himself Latin. Yuck! When Paul grew up he studied science at Cambridge University, England.

In 1912, a giant liner, the *Titanic*, sank after smashing into an iceberg, and over one thousand people drowned. After that catastrophe Langevin became interested in the idea of using sound waves to find a hidden object. He reckoned that sound waves could have been used to spot the iceberg. So in 1915, Langevin developed his idea into the invention later known as SONAR (which stands for SOund NAvigation and Ranging).

A machine called a transducer makes a kind of PING noise (too high for human ears to make out) and the sound waves from this bounce off underwater objects like shipwrecks, shoals of fish, whales, submarines and scuba diving elephants.

SOUND WAVES HIT OBJECT AND BOUNCE BACK

SONAR SENDS SOUND WAVES DOWNWARDS

The echoes are picked up by the transducer and turned into electrical impulses.

A receiver then measures the strength of the echoes and the time they took to reach the ship. The stronger the echo, the more solid the underwater object and the longer it takes to return, the more distant the object. Got all that? You can see the position of the object on a screen and find out how it's moving. Sound idea!

But sadly instead of helping to save lives, Langevin's invention helped to kill people. During the Second World War, SONAR was used to track down enemy submarines so that they could be destroyed with underwater bombs called depth charges.

Then in 1940, the Germans invaded France and Langevin found himself up to his ears in danger. His son-in-law opposed the take-over but he was executed. Then Langevin and his daughter were arrested. Surely, it was only a matter of time before the scientist faced the death penalty. Scientists around the world sent messages of support for Langevin and the Germans decided to lock him up in his own home. But he was still in danger and, helped by some brave friends, he escaped to Switzerland.

Today SONAR is still used to find underwater objects and in 1987 it faced its greatest test. Could SONAR locate the legendary monster in Loch Ness, Scotland? Mention the Loch Ness monster to most scientists and they sigh rather sadly and say, 'Oh, not that old chestnut!'

If there is a monster, say the scientists, how come there's no scientific proof like a dead monster's body? But just imagine there *was* a monster. And just imagine if this super-intelligent, super-sensitive creature could tell its own story? Here's what it might say...

"TROUBLED WATERS"

by Nessie 9-10 October 1987

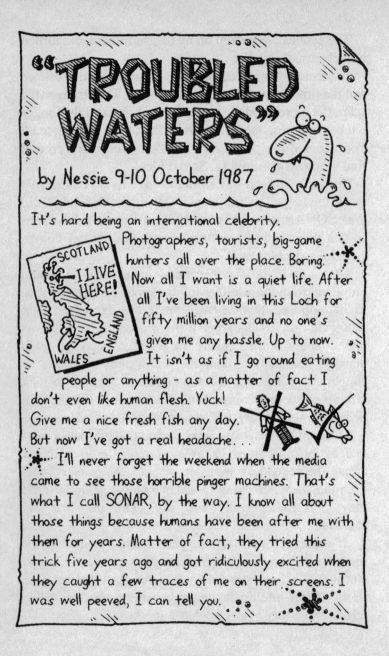

It's hard being an international celebrity. Photographers, tourists, big-game hunters all over the place. Boring. Now all I want is a quiet life. After all I've been living in this Loch for fifty million years and no one's given me any hassle. Up to now. It isn't as if I go round eating people or anything - as a matter of fact I don't even like human flesh. Yuck! Give me a nice fresh fish any day. But now I've got a real headache...

I'll never forget the weekend when the media came to see those horrible pinger machines. That's what I call SONAR, by the way. I know all about those things because humans have been after me with them for years. Matter of fact, they tried this trick five years ago and got ridiculously excited when they caught a few traces of me on their screens. I was well peeved, I can tell you.

SCOTLAND
I LIVE HERE!
WALES   ENGLAND

Of course, I never dreamt they'd try again. I was having a quiet little swim - as you do. I mean, the Loch might be deep and dark and freezing cold and gloomy but it's home to me. Anyway, I poked my head up above water for a quick nose about and that's when I saw them. Hundreds of journalists, dozens of boats, helicopters, TV cameras - the works. You could have knocked me down with a dead haddock. Luckily, they were all listening to a big guy with a bushy beard. Otherwise I'd have been spotted.

Matter of fact, I know the big guy. Adrian Shine is his name. He's a scientist and he's been trying to spot me for years. (Ha, ha, you should be so lucky, Ade.) Anyway, he was telling the pilots of the boats to, "Form a line across the loch and keep on going at a steady speed." Blimey - he even had flags on either bank to keep the boats in line - and those blinkin' pingers. Every boat had one. Noise? Huh, all that pinging all day long - I got a MONSTER headache!

flags

line of boats with SONAR

I know they spotted me a couple of times. I was hiding about 150 metres (411 feet) down. *That should be enough*, I thought. But I should have realized, this stupid SONAR noise goes down hundreds of metres. Anyway, I heard a ping really close and up above they were all *shouting*:

"It's a monster - he's down there!"

He? Blooming cheek - I'm a SHE!

So I beat a hasty retreat. But that night I surfaced and heard people talking - it was a press conference. A couple of American SONAR experts were sounding very puzzled about the signals. One said they don't look as if they've been made by fish.

Fish? Grrr, I'm not a FISH - but what did he know? Anyway, they managed to ping me next day too, but then I made myself really scarce. Didn't want to get myself caught on SONAR again, did I?

I mean, just imagine if they got some real proof that I existed. The autograph hunters, TV wildlife documentaries, royal visits. It's not going to happen. I'm going to skulk in my cosy underwater cave until they've gone home. Yeah, push off humans, can't you see I want to be alone?

Loch Ness – the dreadful truth

The SONAR sweep of Loch Ness covered two-thirds of the vast loch. It had been thorough and well-planned. But the dreadful truth was that it failed to prove Nessie existed. All the scientists had to show for their hard work was a few marks on a sonar chart. The charts were computer print-outs from a sonar screen and the marks showed moving solid objects. Could these be traces of an unknown creature? A large creature bigger than any known type of fish. The file on the Loch Ness monster remains open.

So what would you do if you managed to spot a huge monster unknown to science. Would you...

a) shout for joy
b) say hello
c) scream for your Mummy?

Chances are you'd want to make some kind of sound. Wanna know how? Better clear your throat and read the next chapter.

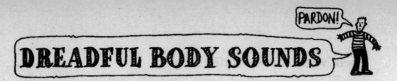

DREADFUL BODY SOUNDS

It's great being you, isn't it? You can make so many smashing noises. Some are musical, some aren't and some are just plain rude. After you make a rude noise have you noticed that that's when your friends make noises, too? Those strange shuddering, tinkling, squeaking, braying sounds we call '"laughter".

Dreadful burps, farts and raspberries
Here's how to make some entertaining body noises, but **don't** make them...
a) In a science lesson

b) In school assemblies or dinner times
c) When the posh relatives come for lunch

Otherwise you'll never hear the end of it.

Farting

Made by vibrating skin around your bottom as air rushes out. You can make similar noises by putting your mouth over your arm and blowing hard.

Snoring

UVULA

Made by the uvula (that's the dangling bit at the back of your throat). If a person sleeps on their back with their mouth open, their deep breathing makes the uvula flutter. You can make a disgusting snoring sound by lying in this position and breathing in.

Bet you never knew!
So you think your dad/uncle/grandad/pet pot-bellied pig snores like a pneumatic drill? Huh – that's nothing! In 1993, Kare Walkert of Sweden was recorded snoring at 93 dB. That's louder than a really noisy disco. By the way, the best thing to do with someone who snores isn't to hit them over the head. No, all you do is gently close their mouths and turn them on their sides. Ahh, peace, perfect peace!

Burping

The air comes up not from your lungs but from your stomach. The vibrations from the gullet (the food passage from your mouth to your stomach) gives the burp its unique and rather endearing tone. To burp, try pushing in your tummy and opening your mouth wide. It helps if you've just scoffed your lunch in five seconds then slurped a fizzy drink.

Whistles and humming

These aren't exactly rude, but I suppose it depends where you do them. For example, it wouldn't be a good idea to whistle the tune to 'The Sound of Music' when you were at church.

Humming is caused partly by a particular set of vibrations in the skin inside the nostrils. Try pinching your nose as you hum and you'll hear how important this is.

Whistles are caused by air whistling though the round hole made by your lips forming little whirlwinds in your mouth that make its inside vibrate.

Talking about vibrating insides, there's lots of fascinating sounds going on inside your body...

Sounds unhealthy

One day in 1751, Austrian doctor Leopold Auenbrugg (1727-1809) happened to notice a wine merchant tapping a barrel. The merchant explained that the sound told him how full the barrel was. *Hmm*, thought the doctor, *I wonder if you could do this for the human body?*

After a lot of thought Leopold wrote a book. He'd figured out a new way to discover if the body was unhealthy. Here's your chance to try it, too.

Dare you discover ... how to hear your own chest?

What you need:

Two tupperware boxes with lids (these represent your chest)

Your hands

What you do:

1 Half fill one box with water.

2 Place the middle finger of your left hand so it's lying flat on the lid of the empty box.

3 Tap the middle portion of this finger with the middle finger of your right hand. The tap should be a smart downwards flick of the wrist.
4 Try to remember the sound.
5 Now repeat steps 1-3 on the lid of the box half full of water.

What do you notice?
a) The two sounds are exactly the same.
b) The empty box makes a dull empty sound and the box with water makes a higher sound.
c) The empty box sounds more hollow, the box with water sounds duller.

Answer: c) Doctors can still use this method to check out what's going on inside your chest. If the chest sounds hollow like a drum it means there is air in the space around the lungs (there should be fluid there).

Dreadful expressions
A doctor tells you…

I'LL HAVE TO DO SOME AUSCULATION

Should you scream and ask for a painkiller?

The stunning stethoscope

For hundreds of years doctors had a simple way to listen to their patients' breathing and heartbeat.

But one day shy French doctor René Laënnec (1781-1826) found himself in an embarrassing situation.

In desperation Laënnec remembered seeing two boys playing with a hollow log. One boy tapped the log and the other listened to the sound at the other end.

So Laënnec figured that a tube might be a good way to hear sounds louder. He rolled up a newspaper.

Success! Laënnec heard the young lady's heartbeat loud and clear. He wrote a book about his new technique and became rich and famous.

Sadly, though, Laënnec fell ill. And the man who had done so much to help doctors treat chest diseases eventually died ... of a chest disease.

Bet you never knew!
By listening through a stethoscope you can find out if a person has a whole range of dreadful diseases. For example, when someone with the lung disease bronchitis (bron-ki-tis), breathes they make a kind of bubbling, crackling noise. Some heartless doctors describe this dreadful sound as "bubble and squeak".

Sounds dreadful fact file

NAME: Your voice

THE BASIC FACTS: The sound waves of a voice are affected by the shape of its owner's skull and mouth, etc. So every voice is different.

THE DREADFUL DETAILS: People who have had their vocal chords removed can still talk. But their voices come out as a whisper.

Here's where your voice comes from...

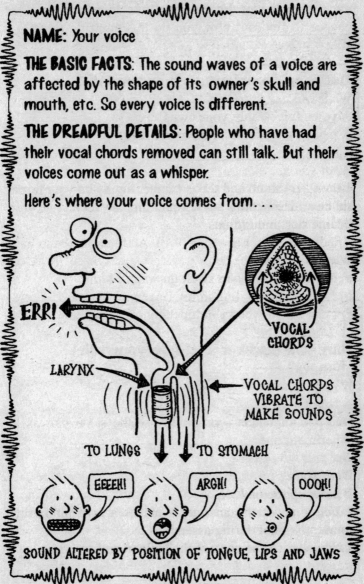

ERR!

VOCAL CHORDS

LARYNX

VOCAL CHORDS VIBRATE TO MAKE SOUNDS

TO LUNGS   TO STOMACH

EEEEH!   ARGH!   OOOH!

SOUND ALTERED BY POSITION OF TONGUE, LIPS AND JAWS

Do you like talking? Sorry, silly question. I mean do ducks like water, do elephants like buns? Here's your chance to find out how you do this amazing thing – a chin-wag.

Dare you discover 1 ... how you talk?
What you need:
A voice (preferably your own)
A pair of hands (preferably your own)

What you do:
1 Put your thumb and second finger lightly on your throat so they are touching but not pressing on it.
2 Now start humming.

What do you notice?
a) My throat seems to swell up when I hum.
b) I can feel a tingling in my fingers.
c) I can't hum when I'm touching my throat.

Dare you discover 2 ... how your voice changes?
What you need:
A balloon
One pair of hands (you could use the same pair as in experiment one)

What you do:
1 Blow up the balloon.
2 Let some of the air out. It makes a brilliant farting sound. (No, not during assembly).
3 Now stretch the neck of the balloon and try again.

What do you notice?
a) No sound comes out.
b) The sound gets higher.
c) The sound gets louder.

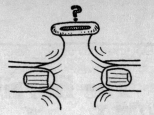

Learn how to talk

OK, so you probably know how to do this anyway.

1 Try saying the letters A, E, I, O, U. Notice anything? The sounds are all made by complex air vibrations in your mouth.

2 Now say S, B, P. Notice what happens to your lips and tongue. Can you feel them moving? Can you say these letters without moving your tongue? Thought not.

3 Say N and M. Notice how part of the sound seems to come out of your nose. Try pinching your nose and notice what happens to the sound.

BY DOSE IS BLOCKED!

Keep going. With more practice you might do as well as these people…

The Horrible Science
Vocal Awards

RUNNER-UP: In 1990, Steve Woodmore of Orpington, England, spoke 595 words in 56.01 seconds. That's roughly all the words from here to page 106. Could you do this?

SECOND PRIZE: In 1988 Analisa Wragg of Belfast, Northern Ireland shouted at 121.7 dB – that's louder than a whole noisy factory. Bet she was cross about something.

CHAMPION: In 1983 Briton Roy Lomas whistled at 122.5 dB. That's louder than a small aircraft engine.

Something to shout about

Have you ever really shouted at someone really loud? I mean at the top of your voice – just as loud as you can. Of course you have. Maybe at the same time you spread your hands on either side of your mouth. Have you noticed how this makes your voice sound louder? A megaphone is only a cone with a hole in one end, but what a difference it makes. Here's how it works.

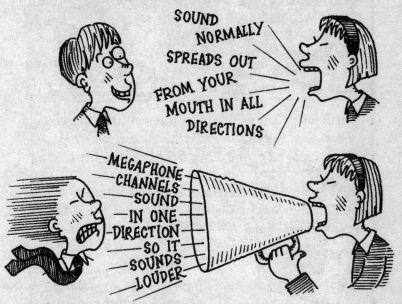

SOUND NORMALLY SPREADS OUT FROM YOUR MOUTH IN ALL DIRECTIONS

MEGAPHONE CHANNELS SOUND IN ONE DIRECTION SO IT SOUNDS LOUDER

Mega-mouth Morland

The megaphone was the brainchild of wacky British inventor Samuel Morland (1625-1695). Sam had an amazing life – it was certainly something to sound off about. As a young man Morland worked for the government. It was a time when Britain was ruled by Oliver Cromwell and King Charles II was in lonely exile in France.

One night Morland overheard his boss and Oliver Cromwell hatching a plot to kill the king. Morland was scared and pretended to be asleep at his desk. Cromwell saw Morland and decided to kill him before he gave away the plot.

But Sam's boss persuaded Cromwell that the young man had been asleep. In 1660 Charles returned to power and Sam convinced the King he'd been on his side all along.

Sam became interested in science and built a powerful pump. He showed it off by squirting water and red wine over the top of Windsor Castle.

And he also invented the megaphone. One day the inventor got in a boat and shouted to the king from a distance of 0.8 km (half a mile). History doesn't record what he said – it might have been something like this...

For hundreds of years the megaphone was the only way to make the human voice carry over large distances. And then someone made a re-sound-ing discovery.

Hall of fame: Alexander Graham Bell (1847-1922), Nationality: British-American

Young Alexander Graham was bound to be fascinated by sound – it ran in the family. His dad was a Scottish professor who taught people with hearing difficulties to speak. This was handy because Alexander's mum also had hearing difficulties.

The young boy had a mind of his own. Aged only 11 he changed his name to Alexander Graham Bell in honour of a family friend. Unfortunately, having a mind of your own wasn't a good idea if you wanted to get on at school. Alexander hated the strict boring lessons. (Does this ring a bell with you?)

Alexander left school without any qualifications and thought about running away to sea. But then he had second thoughts and chose a life involving REAL hardship and deprivation. That's right – he became a teacher. This was quite surprising when you consider he was only 16 at the time – that's younger than some of his pupils. (But he looked older.)

In 1870 Alexander moved with his family to America and got a job teaching deaf children how to speak. Unlike some teachers Alexander was always kind and gentle and he NEVER lost his temper – sounds amazing!

But at nights he worked secretly on another interest. He began to dream of a new machine. A machine that could carry the human voice for hundreds of kilometres. A machine that would change the world for ever.

Could you be a scientist?

As a teenager, Alexander Graham Bell had a sound interest in science. Here are two of his favourite experiments. Can you predict the results?

1 Alexander and his brother built a talking machine. It was made of wood, cotton, rubber, a tin tube for the throat and a real human skull.

Alexander's brother blew air up the model's throat to supply puff to get the voice going. Alexander moved the model lips and tongue to make the noises that we call speech. But would the machine work? What do you think?

a) The model never said a word – just a quiet hissing sound.
b) The model said, "Hi, dad!" in a clear voice. Alexander's dad saw the talking skull and fainted.
c) The model spoke in a Donald Duck-style voice.

2 Alexander decided to help his pet dog talk by moving its jaw and throat. How did he get on?
a) Terrible. The dog refused to say a word.
b) Smashing. Alexander was the first human to have an intelligent conversation with a dog.
c) The dog learnt how to ask, "How are you, grandmama?"

Answers: 1 c) It could say, "Mama". The neighbours heard the voice and wanted to know whose baby it was. **2 c)** Actually the dog said, " Ow ah oo ga ma ma." But Alexander claimed the experiment was a success. And it was these experiments that paved the way to his greatest discovery.

That rings A. Bell

It's actually true that five hundred and ninety-nine people said they invented the telephone before Bell. Five hundred and ninety-eight of them were liars keen to cash in on the phone's success. But one of them, American born Elisha Gray, just happened to be telling the truth.

Elisha Gray was a professional inventor with his own firm part-owned by the Western Union Telegraph Company. He'd been thinking of ways to send sounds along electrical wires and had already made a few successful experiments.

One day in 1875, Gray saw two boys playing with a toy. It was two tin cans linked by a string. One boy would speak into a tin can and the string carried the sound waves to the other can which the other boy held to his ear. A light bulb flashed in the inventor's brain. He came up with an idea for transmitting not just sounds but actual voices along a wire. It was identical to Bell's design even though the two inventors had never met.

Gray managed to sketch out his idea on 11 February – that's a month before Bell put his thoughts on paper. So Gray was now on track to win fame and fortune. But meanwhile Bell and his assistant Thomas Watson were working flat out to build their machine. Their telephone was the result of two years' hard work. Its improvements were based on trial and error. It was made up of…

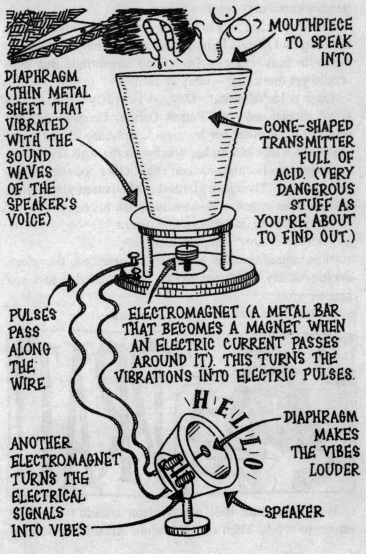

MOUTHPIECE TO SPEAK INTO

DIAPHRAGM (THIN METAL SHEET THAT VIBRATED WITH THE SOUND WAVES OF THE SPEAKER'S VOICE)

CONE-SHAPED TRANSMITTER FULL OF ACID. (VERY DANGEROUS STUFF AS YOU'RE ABOUT TO FIND OUT.)

PULSES PASS ALONG THE WIRE

ELECTROMAGNET (A METAL BAR THAT BECOMES A MAGNET WHEN AN ELECTRIC CURRENT PASSES AROUND IT). THIS TURNS THE VIBRATIONS INTO ELECTRIC PULSES.

HELLO

DIAPHRAGM MAKES THE VIBES LOUDER

ANOTHER ELECTROMAGNET TURNS THE ELECTRICAL SIGNALS INTO VIBES

SPEAKER

The race was on to grab the glory and win the huge cash prizes that would follow from the new technology. But neither inventor knew about the other, remember. So neither knew they were in a race.

The next stage was to file the plans of the invention at the Patent Office. This allows the inventor exclusive rights to make money from their invention. But who would get there first – Gray or Bell?

On a cold Valentine's Day, 14 February 1876, Elisha Gray rushed into the Patent Office. He was eagerly clutching the plans for his new telephone. It was 2 pm precisely. The clock ticked loudly on the wall. The clerk sat writing in his high-backed chair. Gray coughed to get his attention. The clerk glanced at the patent application and then put it down. He slowly shook his head.

"Sorry, sir, I can't accept this patent."

"Why ever not?" snapped Gray.

"I'm afraid you're too late," announced the clerk apologetically. Bell's patent had been handed in just two hours earlier.

"DRAT!" shouted the foiled inventor.

But meanwhile Bell and Watson couldn't get their phone to work. Then on 10 March, Alexander Graham

Bell slopped some acid from the phone speakers on his clothes and made the world's first telephone call by accident.

"Mr Watson, come here I want you!" he yelled, perhaps adding under his breath "and this acid's eating my trousers."

Thomas Watson ran to the aid of his boss whose faint and crackling voice he heard through the strange machine.

This was the call that launched a million chat lines. A defining moment in modern history. But when Bell rang Watson he hadn't rehearsed the words that would change the world, and he hadn't planned to dissolve his pants either.

(Some boring historians point out that Watson didn't get round to telling this story until fifty years later. So was it true? Perhaps. Maybe Watson kept it quiet until then to avoid making his good friend Bell look like a dumb-Bell.)

So Watson got a bell from A. Bell and Elisha Gray was beaten to the bell. In 1877, Gray and the Western Union Telegraph Company took legal action against Bell and his backers claiming that Gray had got to the telephone first. Who would win? Would Bell get his just desserts or would Gray's story ring true with the judge?

What do you think?
a) The judge agreed with Gray. Bell's claim was phone-y and he had to give all his profits to Gray's company, leaving Bell penniless.
b) Gray and Bell agreed to split the money fifty-fifty. It was a fair dial – er, sorry deal.
c) Gray lost and had to call it a day. He didn't get a bean.

Dreadfully successful

The telephone was an instant smash-hit. By 1887 there were 150,000 telephones in the USA alone. For its inventors it was a chance to ring in the profits. But for Alexander Graham Bell personally it was a nightmare come to life. He once said:

Financial dealings are distasteful to me and not at all in my line.

The point was, Bell was happier just being a scientist. So at the ripe old age of 33 he retired to devote the rest of his life to scientific research. And he came up with plenty more inventions including:

• A probe to find bullets stuck in the body.
• An idea for making water from fog.
• A super-fast hydrofoil boat.

Bell loved machines and gadgets but one gadget in

particular got on his nerves: he never allowed a phone near his lab. It was, he said, a distraction from his work.

Bet you never knew!
In the early days of telephones there were attempts to use them to broadcast music. In 1889, a company in Paris used phone lines to broadcast concerts to loudspeakers in hotels. The audience had to put money in the machines to get to the end of the piece. Sounds dreadful.

But it's not as bad as some of the dreadful musical moments you'll find in the next chapter. Can you stand crazy concerts, mad musicians and hideous clashing discords? If not, stuff a big wad of cotton wool in your ears and read on anyway.

It's official! 99.9 per cent of us reckon music is smashing. Yes, great music can make our hearts jump for joy. It makes the world dance and sing, and laugh or even cry with its beauty. And bad music? Well, that's just a pain between the ears.

Could you be a scientist?

A scientist at the University of California, USA, used a computer to show patterns of nerves firing in the brain. His colleague suggested making the computer play the pattern in the form of sounds. And amazingly, these sounded just like classical music. So the scientists wondered whether listening to classical music could actually make the nerves work more effectively. Could the brain work better?

The scientists decided to test the idea by giving three groups of students some tricky questions.

Group 1 had ten minutes of silence before they started.

Group 2 listened to a voice tape designed to make them more relaxed.

Group 3 listened to ten minutes of classical music by Mozart.

Which group did best in the tests?

a) Group 1. Any sound puts the brain off. That's why people need peace and quiet to work.

b) Group 2. The brain is best stimulated by the sound of a human voice.

c) Group 3. The theory was correct!

Answer: c) These students scored 8-9 points above the others. Could this help you in a science test? In 1997 scientists in London found that children aged nine to 11 learn more easily when there's soothing music in the background. So why don't teachers use it to liven up science lessons?

Research shows that listening to music can boost mental performance owing to a similarity between sound waves and nerve signal patterns.

A disgusting din?

Despite the possible brain-boosting powers of music, every musician has had to put up with lots of unkind people who hated their work. It just goes to show that good music like good food is really a matter of taste.

Here's just one example – German composer Richard Wagner (1813-1883). Wagner composed grand and often incredibly loud music for huge orchestras. He had many fans but some people thought Wagner's music was worse than toothache. "Wagner has beautiful moments but awful quarter hours," commented GA Rossini (1792-1868). Other comments on the subject of Wagner's music were:

"I love Wagner, but the music I prefer is that of a cat . . . outside a window and trying to stick to the panes of glass with its claws."

Charles Baudelaire (1821-1867)
Mark Twain (1835-1910) thought Wagner's music sounded dreadful:

". . . at times the pain was so exquisite I could hardly keep the tears back. At those times, as the howlings and wailings and shriekings of the singers and the ragings and roarings and explosions of the vast orchestra rose higher and higher . . . I could have cried."

I expect your music teacher feels the same during school orchestra and school choir practice. And talking about great musicians, are you still itching to become a pop star? Brilliant, 'cos it's time to re-join Jez and Wanda in the sound studio to tackle the next stage of your training – learning to sing. (Admittedly some pop stars don't bother with this bit, but it can help!)

Could you be a pop star? Step 2: Singing

Wanda's just explaining the science of singing:

117

It's actually harder than you might think to become an expert singer, but these few tips should help:

1 First choose a song to practise. It helps if you know the tune and at least some of the words.

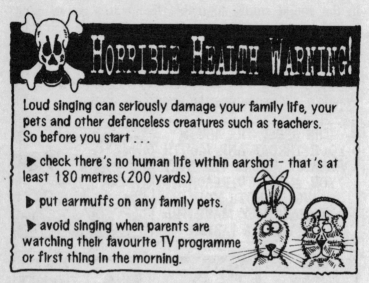

HORRIBLE HEALTH WARNING!

Loud singing can seriously damage your family life, your pets and other defenceless creatures such as teachers. So before you start . . .

▶ check there's no human life within earshot – that's at least 180 metres (200 yards).

▶ put earmuffs on any family pets.

▶ avoid singing when parents are watching their favourite TV programme or first thing in the morning.

2 Stand with your head back and your shoulders back. Breathe in deeply to the pit of your tummy. Easy, innit?

3 Now it gets a bit trickier. Start singing. Carry on with the deep breathing as you sing. Try to open your mouth more widely than you usually do when you speak.

4 You'll find it's easier to produce higher and clearer notes if you smile whilst you sing. Try it and see.

5 OK, that's enough singing. I SAID THAT'S ENOUGH! Now here's the hard bit: singing in tune (some people never get this far). Try singing the same note as a key on the piano or a note on a recorder. Can you get it right? On a piano the keys are arranged in order of pitch. You may know them as...

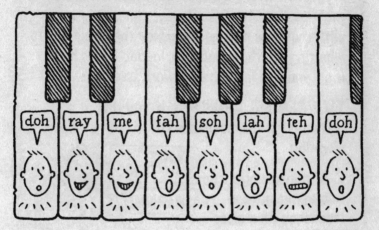

Bet you never knew!
Isn't it amazing you can still hear a singer even when an orchestra is blasting out sound? Surely the roar of all the different instruments ought to drown out the singer's voice? But it doesn't and the reason why is that a trained singer can produce sound at 2,500 Hz – that's five times higher than most of the sound made by the orchestra. So you hear the singer clearly.

But the most amazing musical secret is in the vibes. Yep, we're talking about resonance again ... but *beware* this info could really SHAKE you up.

Sounds dreadful fact file

NAME: Resonance

THE BASIC FACTS: Everything has a natural frequency. That's the speed at which it vibrates most easily. When sound waves hit an object with the same natural frequency the object starts vibrating. So the sound gets louder. This is how most musical instruments work (see page 122).

THE DREADFUL DETAILS: 1 If you sing at a certain pitch the resonance starts your eyeballs vibrating.

2 A trained singer can sing at the natural frequency of a glass and make it vibrate. Some singers can even smash the glass if they sing loudly enough.

WHAT DO YOU THINK?

SMASHING!

LAAH!

Dare you discover ... how to make sounds resonate?

What you need:
A sea shell shaped like this...

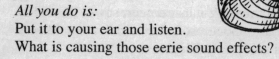

All you do is:
Put it to your ear and listen.
What is causing those eerie sound effects?

a) The ghostly echoes of the sea.

b) It's the sounds around you resonating in the shell.

c) These are faint sounds stored by chemical structures in the shell and released by the heat of your body.

CHECK FIRST THAT NOTHING'S LIVING IN THE SHELL — SORRY, SHOULD HAVE MENTIONED THAT EARLIER

Could you be a pop star? Step 3: Musical instruments

To be a real star it might help to do more than just sing. In fact, why not learn a few instruments so you can really impress your fans? In the sound studio Jez and Wanda are comparing notes on musical instruments.

Strings and things

A stringed instrument is made up of strings stretched tight over an empty case.

ACOUSTIC GUITAR

STRINGS

EMPTY CASE

VIOLIN

DOUBLE BASS

TRADITIONAL VIOLIN STRINGS WERE MADE FROM DRIED CAT'S GUTS

YIKES!

123

Dreadful expressions

A scientist says…

I'VE ALWAYS WANTED A CHORDOPHONE (KOR-DO-FONE) LIKE THIS

Can you really buy chord phones that look like violins?

Answer: No. A chordophone is the posh term for a stringed instrument like the violin. It means " stringed sound" in Greek. By the way, woodwind instruments are aerophones (air-ro-fones) (not aeroplanes – dimwit), brass instruments and drums are membranophones (mem-brain-o-fones) and percussion instruments are idiophones (i-deo-fones). No, that doesn't mean that they're played by idiots – even if these instruments seem easier to play.

A quick musical interlude

You've probably seen someone "tickling the ivories" of a piano before. You might even have had a go yourself. But did you know that the piano is also a type of stringed instrument? Here's how it works…

1 Press a key on the piano and you set in motion a series of levers.
2 The levers lift a hammer that strikes a tightly stretched wire to sound the note.

But things can go wrong. For example, damp air can make the felt between the piano keys take in moisture and swell up. The keys stick together and the pianist plays two notes instead of one. Then you get dreadful scenes of mayhem. This is what really happened at the Erawan Hotel in Bangkok, Thailand…

CONTINUED

You'll be pleased to know that Mr Kropp was stopped from totally wrecking the piano by the Hotel Manager, two security guards and a passing police officer. If you're having piano lessons I hope this doesn't give you any ideas.

Warbling wind instruments

To make a really mellow sound you'll probably need more than just stringed instruments. How about adding a few woodwind instruments to your line up? A funky saxophone, a cool clarinet or a soulful flute.

Note: Woodwind instruments were once made from wood – that's how they get their name. Now they're often made from metal or other materials.

Wanda has volunteered to show us how to play a few wind instruments. Ever tried to play a milk bottle? That's a bit like blowing into a flute. You need to blow across the top:

BLOWING OVER THE HOLE MAKES THE AIR IN THE FLUTE VIBRATE

SPLUTTER!

DRIBBLE!

Well, in theory the air inside the flute vibrates to make the sound. In a saxophone or clarinet a reed in the mouthpiece vibrates when you blow to get the same effect.

WHEEZE!

COVERING THE HOLES STOPS THE AIR ESCAPING AND ALTERS THE NOTE

PUFF!

VIBRATING REED MAKES AIR INSIDE THE SAXOPHONE VIBRATE

A deeper sound comes out. Larger things make a lower sound when they vibrate, remember.

Brilliant brass

A fanfare of trumpets would really add some oomph to your hit. Brilliant brass instruments include…

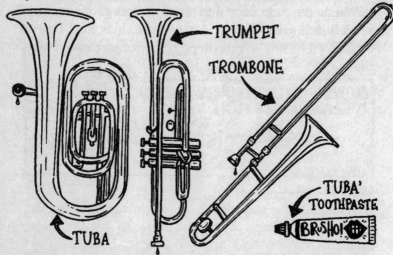

Like woodwind instruments you get the sound from air vibrating inside the instrument. But the vibes come from the special way you move your lips. By blowing a raspberry – here's Wanda's attempt.

As with woodwind instruments, covering the holes makes the sound lower. The longer the pipe the deeper the sound.

Teacher's tea-time teaser

Are you feeling brave? Now's your chance to sound your teacher out on a vital scientific question. Hammer boldly on the staff room door and when it grinds open smile sweetly and say:

I WAS JUST WONDERING WHY YOUR KETTLE HISSES WHEN IT'S JUST ABOUT TO BOIL AND STOPS WHEN THE WATER IS BOILING?

GROAN!

Answer: Hopefully, your teacher will not be boiling with anger at this interruption. The answer to your question is like a wind instrument, the sound is caused by vibrating air. Bubbles rise in the water as it heats up and collapse as they get to the surface. The air vibrates in the kettle and makes the sounds you hear. When the water has boiled the bubbles don't collapse and the sound stops.

Peculiar percussion

Percussion instruments include anything that you can bash together to make sounds. Like…

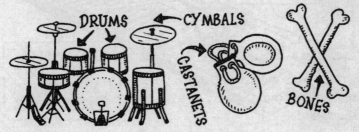

DRUMS — CYMBALS

CASTANETS

BONES

129

Now how about a serious drumbeat? It'll give a great rhythm to your track. It's easy to make a sound on the drums – you just hit them with drumsticks. (No, not chicken drumsticks.)

DRUM VIBRATES AND SO DOES THE AIR INSIDE

LOUDER SOUND COMES OUT

YOU'RE WRONG MAN – CHICKEN DRUMSTICKS ARE COOL!

OK that's enough, Jez.

Bet you never knew!
Can't decide which instrument to play? Just imagine an awesome machine that can make the sound of any instrument in the world. Impossible? No it's really true – it's called a synthesizer.

This is what it looks like:

WHAT D'YOU THINK WANDA?

THAT'S COOL, MAN – ER, I MEAN THAT'S SPLENDID, JEZ

Here's how to use it:

1 It's amazing, you just set the controls for the type of instrument you want to play.

2 The synthesizer makes electronic signals that get stronger and weaker just like the sound waves of the instrument you want to copy.

3 The signals go to an amplifier and are turned into sounds. The sounds are strangely similar to your chosen instrument.

4 The synthesizer has keys so you can play it like a piano. But it can sound very different.

Super samplers and mixing

Playing music was fun but here's the tricky bit. You've got to record the various instruments and mix the tracks together. Jez can do this with the help of a fantastic brain-boggling machine. Or more accurately *two* fantastic mind-boggling machines in one.

The mixer allows Jez to record, or dub, the sound of your voice over the sound of the instruments.

The sampler part of the machine can take ANY sound – an annoying yowling cat for example – and play it back at a different speed. The sampler makes a sound more echoey; it can even play sound backwards. With a sampler your singing will sound even more brilliant.

So how do you feel? Are you bursting to make a big noise? Or in need of a nice cup of tea and a couple of headache pills? Jez and Wanda will be back with some even more serious sound machines later. But for now, keep your earplugs firmly in place. 'Cos the next chapter is LOUD and it really does sound *dreadful*.

TINKLE! **PLINK!** **PLONK!** **BUZZ!** **CRASH!**

DREADFUL SOUND EFFECTS

Here's what you've been waiting for – the chance to blow your own trumpet ... and everything else too. You don't need posh and expensive instruments to make your own music. The good news is you can make interesting and rather horrible sound effects using everyday objects.

Odd orchestra quiz

Musicians have used some really strange things and some really dreadful things to make "musical" instruments. Which of these "instruments" has never been played in a public performance? TRUE/FALSE

1. AN ANIMAL'S BLADDER BAGPIPES

2. A RADIO (NOT TUNED TO ANY STATION)

3. FLOWERPOT DRUMS

4. A HUMAN SKULL RATTLE

5. A PAIR OF FALSE TEETH CASTANETS

Now it's your turn...

Dreadful everyday instruments

Take some milk or other glass bottles for example...
(Actually, it's best if you polish off the contents first.)

Playing a lemonade bottle

1 Drink (slurp)

134

Dare you discover ... how to play bottles?

What you need:
Three identical bottles
Some water
A spoon

All you do is:
1 Fill a bottle with 2.5 cm (1 inch) of water.
2 Puff a short breath across its rim. The sound you hear is the air inside vibrating up and down.
3 Half-fill another bottle with water.
4 Puff across its rim as before.
What do you notice?
a) The sound is higher from the nearly empty bottle.
b) The sound is lower from the nearly empty bottle.
c) The sound is much louder in the half empty bottle.

Now try this...
What you do:
1 Fill the third bottle three-quarters full with water.
2 Line the bottles up in a row.
3 Tap each one with a spoon.

What do you notice?
a) The sound is higher from the nearly empty bottle.
b) The sound is lower in the nearly empty bottle.
c) When you tap the bottles water splashes everywhere.

Krazy kazoos

Kazoos make an interesting if slightly weird sound. Here's how to make your own.

What you need:
A piece of greaseproof paper
A comb

What you do:
1 Fold the greaseproof paper round the comb as shown.
2 Press your lips to the side of the kazoo as shown.
3 Here's the tricky bit. Put your lips together so they're only just open and try humming a tune. The air should be blowing out of your mouth and making the paper vibrate.
4 The wacky sound effects are made by the vibrating paper.

Bet you never knew!
The largest kazoo in the history of the universe was made in New York in 1975. It was 2.1 metres (7 feet) high – that's taller than a door and 1.3 metres (4.5 feet) wide – that's as wide as a small car. It's definitely a BAD IDEA to make your kazoo this big.

Ruler rackets
What you need:
One 30 cm (12 inch) ruler (either wood or plastic)
A table

What you do:
1 Place the ruler half on and half off the table. Hold it in place with one hand on the table.
2 Flick the free end of the ruler with your other hand.

3 You can experiment with different lengths of ruler off the table to make different notes. You'll find that you hear deeper notes when more of the ruler is off the table. Yep, you got it, it's all to do with that larger area vibrating more slowly and making a lower sound.

HORRIBLE HEALTH WARNING!

Don't be tempted to play your ruler during a science lesson. Otherwise your teacher might be tempted to play the ruler, too – using you as a sounding board!

Sonic spoons

Spoons can make some brilliant sounds. The easiest way to do this is to bash two spoons together. This is best done in the privacy of your own home and not in the school canteen. Please note: I did say knock spoons together and not to knock the spoon on...

a) Any nearby priceless ornaments. This could have an effect you'll live to regret.

WHOOPS!

CRACK

b) Your teacher's head. The effects of this on you would be too painful to mention.

Super spoon stereo systems

If you want to experience vibrant spoon sounds in stupendous stereo try this high-tech method. Go on, it's dreadfully awesome.

What you need:
Some string
A metal spoon

LIKE THIS!

What you do:
1 Tie some string round the metal spoon as shown.
2 Press the ends of the strings to the opening of your ear holes. Allow the spoon to bang against a tabletop. (No, I don't mean the objects in **a)** and **b)** above.) Incredible sound effect – isn't it? Solid objects like the string are very good at carrying sound waves, remember? That's why you can hear the various sounds made by the vibrating spoon amazingly well.
3 Try holding the spoon by one string whilst tapping it gently with a metal spoon. You could even try playing a tune.
4 Try experimenting with different sized spoons and metal objects such as metal colanders, egg tongs, etc.

Dreadful sound effects

Of course, there's much more to sounds than making noise. How about making scary sound effects too? You could try recording them on tape to see how effective they are. Then see if your friends can guess what each one is.

A hideous squeak

Rub a piece of polystyrene on a window. The squeaks you hear are actually sound waves caused as tiny lumps on the polystyrene rub quickly over bumps on the glass. Remember – don't make these noises at the wrong moment or you'll hear some hideous squeaks from your family too!

A horrible giant fly

What you need:
An old cereal bag (that's the waxy bag inside a cereal packet)
A glass
A fly

What you do:
1 Catch a fly by putting a plastic glass over it. Be gentle – remember flies have feelings too.
2 Quickly put the cereal bag under the glass and gently

shake the fly into it.

3 Hold the bag to your ear. The fly's footsteps and buzzing resonates in the bag and it sounds seriously dreadful.

4 After you've finished let the fly go outside. After all this is no ordinary hairy little fly – it's a hairy little sound-effect superstar.

A phantom tweet
What you need:
Half a used matchstick
40 cm (16 inches) of thin string
A small cottage cheese carton and lid
A pair of scissors
Sellotape

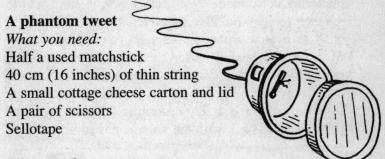

What you do:
1 Cut a 1 cm (0.4 inch) wide hole in the side of the carton.
2 Ask for help to make a small hole in the bottom of the carton – just wide enough for the string to go through.
3 Tie one end of the string to the matchstick. Place the matchstick inside the carton and thread the string through the hole in its bottom.
4 Tape the lid in place on the carton.
5 Swing the carton on the string around your head to make a ghostly tweeting sound.

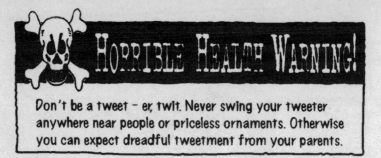
Striking sound effects

The incredible thing about the human brain is, not only can we hear sounds but we instantly know what they are. We can remember them from the first time we heard them. So you can recognize the curious choking spluttering noise made by a teacher who is just about to lose their temper and dive for cover.

If you listen to a play on the radio you will hear sound effects for things going on in the play. So how sound is your judgement? Can you match the sound effect to the way it's produced? You won't be disqualified for trying the sound effects out. Try recording them on tape and then play them back with the volume turned up.

1 A GALLOPING HORSE

2 A SLAP ROUND THE CHOPS

3 RAIN BEATING ON A ROOF

4 FOOTSTEPS ON A GRAVEL DRIVE

5 A COLLAPSING HOUSE

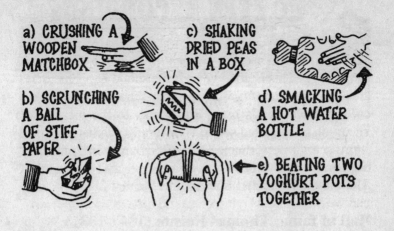

a) CRUSHING A WOODEN MATCHBOX

c) SHAKING DRIED PEAS IN A BOX

b) SCRUNCHING A BALL OF STIFF PAPER

d) SMACKING A HOT WATER BOTTLE

e) BEATING TWO YOGHURT POTS TOGETHER

Answers: 1 e), 2 d), 3 c), 4 b), 5 a)

If you had a go at recording those sounds, you probably won't be surprised to hear that these sound effects have all been recorded for use in radio plays. And if you want to find out more about the weird world of recorded sound, just press the button and tune in to the next chapter.

READ ON AND BE AMAZED!

No sound lasts for ever – it dies away as the vibrations lose energy. This is good news if the sound happens to be dreadful. No matter how rotten your school concert solo, once it's over – it's over. But thanks to the incredible invention of recorded sound your family can listen to the entire school performance full of embarrassing hiccups, raspberries and screeches over and over and over again. ARRGGGGGGGHHH! So who's to blame?

Hall of fame: Thomas Edison (1847-1931)
Nationality: American

Young Thomas or Al as he was called (from Alva, his middle name) was useless at school. (Now where have we heard that before?) Al's teacher told him…

And told his mum…

Actually, what no one seemed to realize was young Al couldn't hear too well. So he couldn't hear his teachers clearly. Lucky for him, considering the cruel things they said. But it was even luckier that Al's parents were kind and understanding. They took their son away from school and taught him at home. "Luck!" I hear you say. "Sounds more like a miracle to me!"

Al loved it. He turned his dad's wood yard into a chemistry lab and burnt it down when an experiment went wrong. At the age of ten he set up another chemistry lab in the basement. This was the scene for loads of dreadfully fascinating experiments that generally resulted in horrible smells, burnt clothes and wrecked furniture.

Then, at the age of 12, Al decided to get a job and started work selling newspapers and drinks on local trains. This gave him lots of time to convert the baggage carriage into a mobile chemistry lab resulting in ... you guessed it ... horrible smells, burnt clothes and wrecked furniture.

Young Al wasn't cut out to be a newspaper seller. (His destiny lay as an inventor and a scientist.) His next job was working as a telegraph clerk on his own each night.

But he found the job really tedious so he invented a machine that sent a special telegraph signal every hour to show his bosses he was still awake – while he slept. The machine worked perfectly until one night an incoming signal came in while Al was in the land of Nod. He'd hit the sack and as a result he got it – the sack that is.

For a while Al drifted from job to job. He wore scruffy clothes and rarely washed and didn't care what he ate. (Know anyone like that?) He often worked at night so he could spend the day doing scientific experiments. His big break came in New York.

He was snoozing in a friend's office because he had nowhere else to stay when the stock ticker broke. This was a kind of telegraph used to send financial information. Of course, Al was a telegraph wizard, and he fixed the machine and made it work better than before. The company bosses were so impressed that they offered Al a job.

In fact, the Western Union Telegraph Company also took an interest in the bright young man and offered him a huge contract to invent an improved telegraph. Could you achieve this kind of success? How would you measure up against the great Edison?

Thomas Edison quiz

Imagine you are Thomas A. Edison. All you need to do is decide how you would act in each situation.

1 You have a technical problem with an urgent order for stock tickers. How do you solve it?

a) You lock the lab and send everyone on holiday until the problem is solved. (People have good ideas on holiday.)

b) You lock your entire staff in the lab until the problem is solved.

c) You lock yourself in the lab for sixty hours without food until the problem is solved.

2 You have a serious scientific problem to tackle. What do you do?

a) Call a meeting of your scientific staff and argue the question over. Make sure everyone has their say.

b) Shut yourself in a cupboard and stay there until you think of an answer.

c) Make your staff undertake dangerous experiments to prove your theories.

3 In 1871 you marry a young lady called Mary Sitwell. How do you spend your wedding day?

a) You take the week off work.

b) You go to the wedding but spend the rest of the day at the lab working on science problems.

c) You spend the whole day at the lab and ask your best man to stand in for you at the wedding.

4 You decide to improve the telephone. The acid-filled speaker invented by Alexander Graham Bell wasn't that good at picking up sounds. You look around for an alternative and discover that carbon granules are ideal for passing on the sound waves. How many substances do you test first?

a) 200 **b)** 2,000 **c)** 20,000

Answers: b) is the right answer for all the questions. Please note **2b)** is an unhealthy thing to do so don't try it.

What your answers mean.

All **bs** – congratulations you'd make a great inventor.

All **as** – you're far too laid back. Better get someone to pour you a nice cold drink while you read this book.

All **cs** – you're far too tough and too hard on everyone including yourself. Never mind – you could always become a teacher.

During the 1870s Edison made a series of brilliant inventions. After working on the telephone he became interested in the idea of storing and passing on sound waves, and in 1877 he made an unheard-of discovery.

The phonograph, as it was called, was a massive success. When one of Edison's workers took a machine to show the French Academy of Science, the scientists were so thrilled that they wanted to spend the rest of the evening playing with it.

Bet you never knew!
Amongst the weird and wacky inventions inspired by the phonograph was a talking watch made by a Mr Sivan of Geneva, Switzerland. The watch contained a tiny phonograph that called out, "WAKE UP, GET UP!" first thing in the morning. Edison himself invented a talking doll containing a phonograph that said, "Mama" or "Papa" and told stories.

Trouble was, those fragile foil cylinders really did fall apart after a couple of plays. Other inventors developed phonographs that used wax cylinders instead of foil, and then, after 1888, discs on a flat turntable. The gramophone was born.

Of course, the march of technology has moved on
dramatically since those far off prehistoric days when
your parents were rather less crinkly than they are today.
When you hit the big time you'll have some brilliant
machines to play your latest sounds. Want to find out
more?

Could you be a pop star? STEP 4: Serious sound machines

Once you've recorded your first single you're sure to
want to listen to it again and again. And get your friends
to listen to it too and even their mums and dads, pet
gerbils, etc. So what sort of sound system will show you
in the best possible light? Jez and Wanda are back again
to help you decide.

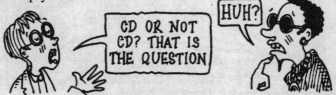

Classic cassette player

Jez is fiddling with this cassette recorder. This machine turns sound into magnetic signals and back again. Sounds incredible, doesn't it?

SOUND CAUSES THE RECORDING HEAD TO MAKE A MAGNETIC SIGNAL

WOOF!

MIKE PICKS UP SOUND WAVES

THE SIGNAL MAKES A PATTERN OF MAGNETIC BITS ON THE TAPE

And now Wanda's going to demonstrate what happens when you play a tape.

MAGNETIC BITS ON THE TAPE HEAD FIRE ELECTRICAL PULSES

WOOF!

AMPLIFIER TURNS THE PULSES INTO SOUNDS THAT MAKE UP THE DOG'S WOOF

The most famous cassette tape player in the world is the Walkman. This was invented by Sony Shibuara President, Akio Morita. (Oh, so you've already got one?) Seems Akio was a keen golfer and music fan and he wanted to listen to music as he played golf. The result – a small cassette machine or CD player with earphones instead of a speaker. So you can listen while you do other things.

Jez and Wanda are investigating a CD player. A CD stores sounds as tiny pits on its surface. The CD player turns these into electrical signals … here's what happens.

When Jez plays the CD disc it spins round mega fast…
And here's where it gets really technical…

Look inside the CD player and you'll find how to turn the pulses back into sounds.

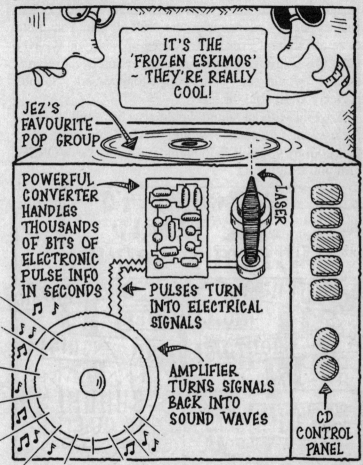

If it all works the CD player produces better sound quality than the tape. Tapes can get twisted or dirty which spoils the sound quality. But the laser beam only picks up the pits on the CD rather than any bits of grease or fluff on its surface.

⚡ SOUNDING IT OUT ⚡

Imagine (if you can) a world without sound. Peace, perfect peace – silence is golden, and all that. You could doze off without ever being woken up, and you'd never have to sit through another science lesson because your teacher would be completely tongue-tied. Sounds perfect? Well, hold on...

A world without sound would also be a dull, lifeless, joyless kind of a place. It would be a bit like having to go to school by yourself in the holidays – only far WORSE. Can you imagine it?

There'd be no games of football (can you imagine a totally quiet game?), no chatting on the phone, no one telling jokes, and definitely NO rude noises. There'd be NO FUN. Nothing but a vast horribly gloomy silence. Sounds dreadful. Could you bear it?

OK, you can turn the volume up again now, and appreciate some of the good sounds you can tune into…

And every year brings sensational sound discoveries… Time was when the most thrilling sound experience you could look forward to was listening to your grandad tinkling a dodgy old piano and singing awful old songs. Nowadays you can listen to whatever you want, whenever you want, and you can pick up a phone and natter to people on the other side of the world.

But sound science discoveries aren't just for fun…
At this very minute scientists are working on new and incredible sound discoveries. Discoveries that will make it easier for people to keep in contact and find out new information. Here are a few that we're already using…

Supersonic sound signals
• Optical fibres send signals as pulses of light to be made into sounds by a phone. So your voice can be turned into an incredible flashing light code. It's then turned back into sound waves so the person on the other end of the

phone can understand you.

• Video phones transmit not only the sound of your voice but also live pictures of you talking. (This could be embarrassing if someone called when you were on the toilet.)

• A computer can actually chat to you. Here's how…

1 Someone speaks words into a machine that turns sound into electronic pulses.

2 These pulses are stored as codes in the computer's vast memory.

3 When the computer speaks the codes are turned back into pulses.

4 And these are converted into sounds which come out of the computer's speakers.

And sounds can even make people *healthier*.

Stunning surgical sound systems

• Ultrasound pulses blast kidney stones. The vibrations break up the painful stones but don't harm the wobbly flesh that surrounds them. Pow!

• Ultrasound scans can produce SONAR-style pictures of unborn babies inside their mums. The picture can be used to check that the babies are OK.

EVERYTHING'S FINE, SHE'S GIVING US THE THUMBS UP!

Sometimes science seems boring, and at times the boring bits can sound really dreadful. But outside the classroom there's a great big world bursting with sound. A huge exciting vibrant world alive with loud, shocking, shrieking, spectacular noises, and thanks to science it's getting more amazing all the time.

The future sounds dreadfully exciting, doesn't it?

HORRIBLE SCIENCE

Science with the squishy bits left in!

Also available:
Ugly Bugs
Why do flies throw up on your tea? Take a magnifying glass to the insect world.

Blood, Bones and Body Bits
Are you dying to find out which animals live on your eyelashes? The human body goes under the scalpel.

Chemical Chaos
What would make the worst stink bomb in the world ever? Discover the smelly side of science.

Nasty Nature
Why do vultures have bald heads? Explore the nasty side of the animal world.

Fatal Forces
Fancy sleeping on a bed of nails? Find out how it's done – without becoming a human pin cushion.

Look out for:
Vicious Veg
Ever wondered what stops trees from falling over? Read up on the world of plants and make your friends go green with envy!

Science has never been so horrible!